The WATERFALL CONCEPT

A blueprint for addiction recovery

By **Roger Stark**
Addiction Counselor

SILVER STAR PUBLISHING

Silver Star Publishing

Silver Star Publishing
P.O. Box 1554
Brush Prairie, WA 98606

Printed in the United States of America

Cover design: Scott Jarrard
Cover photo: Susan Lynn Stark

ISBN: 978-0-615-40125-6

To Susan and our seven children:
Thank you, thank you, thank you.

CONTENTS

PREFACE

*T*he seeds of this book were sown in the depths of my addiction. In that desperate time, the understanding came to me that I was in very serious trouble, but, at the same time, dawned the awful realization that I was completely unaware of what the solution might be. My conscious decision to try to figure out recovery was followed by a prayer, asking for help—a prayer in which I promised I would share with others whatever I learned.

Throughout my journey to recovery, in the educational curriculum which qualified me to work as an addiction counselor, and in the work that I have done as a clinician in the field, I have been taught. What I have come to understand is presented here.

I have written this book with the hope that someone's recovery might be aided, that the suffering of some might be mitigated. The beginning of recovery, and the sometimes long journey, is a very confusing place. This work is presented with the desire that hope may be encouraged and recovery successfully accomplished. It is my greatest desire that this collection of thoughts, rules, guidelines and benchmarks can help. This is the book I wish I had had in those dark days.

CHAPTER 1

The Waterfall Concept

*A*s our seven children were growing up, my wife and I searched for activities that would be fun and interesting for each of them, across the wide age range the seven of them spanned. Somehow, whitewater rafting sounded like a good enough idea that we bought and outfitted a 14-foot raft and prepared for whitewater. After several floats on our local river—a river that did have water, but not much that was white—we went looking for some real adventure. We found ourselves launching onto the Deschutes River in central Oregon, a whitewater haven by any standards. Rapids with names like Boxcar, Oak Springs and Little Wapinita drew crowds of rafters and provided plenty of whitewater excitement. The guidebook I obtained to prepare for the trip also warned of Shearers Falls, a life-threatening Class VI waterfall that lay just after the takeout point.

I wanted no part of that waterfall. I made up my mind that we would be getting out of the water long before the pull of the falls could overtake my young, inexperienced crew. It was very difficult for me to judge where we actually were in relation to the falls, even though I had practically memorized the guidebook. I'm not sure if it was my instincts or my fear that landed us on the shore nearly a quarter mile above the standard takeout point. I didn't mind the extra walking to get to our ride; we were safe and we survived.

There were places along our float where I didn't fear the falls. Just below the Class IV Oak Springs rapid, we went through a huge eddy. The calm water was the signal for the start of a rather intense game of "King of the Raft." Ultimately, we all ended up out of the boat, swimming in the river. Even though I was still worried about the falls downriver, I felt no danger in these waters. Here, the river was still or was moving upstream. The pull of the falls could have no claim on us here. This was a safe place.

In contrast, the area near the precipice of any waterfall is not a safe place. It is at that point, that the river is constricted, gaining speed and power. No individual could stand at the top of Shearers Falls—or any similar waterfall—without being pulled over into the life-threatening torrent below. Only by moving upstream can we be beyond the reach of danger. Upstream, beyond the pull of the falls, inside the waters of the eddies, is where we find our safety.

So it is with addictions. We cannot stand at the precipice of acting out, where our compulsion has its greatest power and strength, and expect our sobriety to survive. We will be pulled into the abyss, losing control, yet again, to our addictive behaviors. We must move upstream to safety. We must move our thoughts and behaviors upstream to safe waters, away from the power and pull of our addiction.

The *White Book*, published by Sexaholics Anonymous, recounts the statement of a long-time addict, who said: *I don't need help quitting, I have quit a thousand times! I need help STAYING QUIT!* (SA 2002). Yet, even knowing the pull and power of addiction, some try to focus recovery work on how to survive while standing at the precipice of the falls (the art of white-knuckling). Instead, counselors, therapists, families— and especially addicts themselves—should be concerned with how to help struggling individuals to stay upstream, in safe waters.

Moving thoughts and behaviors upstream helps addicts "stay quit" and protects them from the addiction waterfalls. These upstream, calm waters are the Waters of Recovery. Finding them, and learning to stay in them, is healing from addiction.

Trying to overcome addiction by white-knuckling is similar to Hood's experience at Gettysburg. Confederate General John Bell Hood led an assault on Union forces through an area called Devil's Den, hoping to take Little Round Top. The ground at Devil's Den is populated with massive boulders, making any military maneuver very difficult. Hood's forces were repulsed, and Hood, himself, wounded. Lying in a field hospital, he reported to General James Longstreet, saying, "It was the worst ground I ever saw."

As addicts, we don't want to be fighting our addiction on bad ground. We want to find where we can be successful. Addiction is best confronted in the safe Waters of Recovery. That is the battlefield where we can obtain victory. Many addicts who are moving into sobriety continue to embrace addictive behaviors or elements of their addiction, then they wonder why recovery eludes them. They are still too close to the falls. Those addictive behaviors are like the boulders Hood encountered; if we hold on to them, our attack on our addiction becomes very, very difficult. We end up losing, yet again, to our enemy of acting out.

When we are in the Waters of Recovery, we are truly, "out of our addiction." We are safe. We are free from the pull of the falls. We practice the thoughts and behaviors of recovery and healing. However, as life—like the river—flows, we must work to maintain our safe position. When our thoughts and behaviors cross that safe dividing line into flowing water, we again find ourselves "in our addiction" and susceptible to the building power of the waterfalls.

The Problem Addicts Have With Blindness

When we are "in our addiction," we are blind to it. Robert Larson MD, puts it this way:

Alcoholism and all other addictions come with built in denial. The patient does not know that they are ill. They have no real concept of how severe the situation is and they are frequently not willing to talk about it at all (Larson 1998).

Denial makes recovery a bit difficult. In the mind of the addict who is in denial, recovery just isn't necessary. The addict's response when first confronted with his situation is: I DO NOT HAVE A PROBLEM! It is an emphatic response, often with anger and indignation that such a thing might even be proposed. The more anger and indignation a person shows, the greater the probability that he has a problem. One of the many painful frustrations for family and friends is watching someone they love, who is losing their life to addiction but seems completely unaware of it.

The Big Book of Alcoholics Anonymous (AA) describes alcoholism as a *cunning and baffling disease* (Bill W, 2001). Indeed, all addictions may be so described. Addictions steal our sense of, and contact with, reality. Part of our blindness comes from our weaving such an intricate web of rationalizations and justifications to allow our addictive behavior that we become engulfed by the darkness of our lies of denial. Drunkenness is excused as, "Just letting off a little steam." Smoking marijuana as, "It's the only thing that helps me relax." We use Meth not because we are addicts but, as we say, "I have to work two jobs and need the help staying awake." The truth is this: *WE ARE ADDICTS. WE DO NOT REALIZE WE ARE ADDICTS, AND WE WILL DO WHATEVER WE HAVE TO DO, AND SAY WHATEVER WE HAVE TO SAY, TO CONTINUE TO BE ADDICTS.*

The Parable of the Unwise Bee illustrates the addict's dilemma. Recounted by Elder James E. Talmage, an early General Authority of the Church, the parable tells the story of a bee that flew into Elder Talmage's office on a warm summer day. The bee flew around the room, looking for a way out, but the insect's efforts failed to find the partly opened window through which it had entered. Seeing the bee's struggle, Elder Talmage took compassion and threw the window open wide and tried to encourage it to fly to safety. He knew that if the bee remained trapped in the room, it would die, but the harder he tried to guide the bee to the window, the angrier and more threatening it became. Elder Talmage says he tried even harder, until the angry bee even stung his hand, "the hand that would have guided it to freedom." The bee persisted in its wild flight and never found its way to freedom. When Elder Talmage returned to his office three days later, he found the bee without life, lying on the desk.

Elder Talmage says:

To the bee's shortsightedness and selfish misunderstanding I was a foe, a persistent persecutor, a mortal enemy bent on its destruction; while in truth

I was its friend, offering it ransom of the life it had put in forfeit through its own error, striving to redeem it, in spite of itself, from the prison-house of death and restore it to the outer air of liberty (Zodell, 1973).

How then, are the blind rescued? How does recovery come to those who are blind to their own addiction and blind to the help they are offered as well? It is a process that begins with understanding.

About What Addiction Is

We don't need a complete, clinical understanding of addiction in order to recover, but we do need to understand enough to become equipped to fight and overcome it. We need the kind of knowledge that will help demystify some of the attendant behaviors and emotions and give us valuable information about our enemy. We need to know how addiction works within us, where we are weak and where we are strong, and how to build a sustainable recovery plan.

Stephanie Brown, PhD, states:

Addiction is loss of control. Addiction is the inability to predictably and consistently stop drinking, using drugs, eating, gambling, acting out sexually or other behaviors once started. Addiction is more than a behavior. Addiction starts with an emotional attachment, or relationship if you will. An emotional bond is formed to alcohol, prescription drugs, food, gambling, etc., that becomes a compulsive attachment. He or she cannot do without it. The object of the addiction becomes the best friend, lover, and the demon that will destroy the addict. Stated another way, addiction becomes a deep loss of self.

Addiction can occur in whatever generates significant mood alteration (Brown 2006). This means not only drugs and alcohol can be the culprits, but the self-nurturing of food, the thrill of gambling, or the arousal of sex can also initiate addiction within us. The emotional bond is formed through the conditioning process that takes place in the emotional center of our brain.

Our brain's emotional center is charged with finding solutions to our human needs. Emotions were given to us to guide us in meeting those needs. The center is always looking for ways to comfort difficult feelings.

The healthy way to do that is in our relationships with others, where we can love and be loved, and feel importance and accomplishment. If this proves unsuccessful, some turn to counterfeit relationships that offer temporary comfort, but not fulfillment. When we chose to be comforted from difficult feelings by using our drug of choice, the emotional bond or connection between the feeling and acting out is reinforced or strengthened. The process clinicians call *conditioning*. When the bond is sufficiently strong, whenever the emotional center feels the need or emotion, an urge is sent out to indulge in our drug of choice.

Upon continued use and, therefore, further conditioning, the connection between our originating emotion and our form of acting out is strengthened to the point that the urge becomes a compulsion. At this point, the ante has been raised. At the compulsive stage of our use, we find that the urge to use is now stronger than our will to resist. Our control of self, the ability to think and chose our reaction has been impaired, hijacked by the emotional center. It has gained the ability to out vote, and begins to control/overrule, the thinking part of our brain. We can no longer just say no. We have compromised our freedom to choose, and we are in trouble—big trouble.

Part of the emotional center's purpose is to handle emergencies. If we put our hand on the hot stove, it is not the thinking part of our brain that tells us to move our hand, but rather, it is the emotional center. Thinking is bypassed because of the emergency nature of the situation. In such instances, the emotional center can trump the rest of the brain to protect us from danger. Our thinking brain suspends control or steps aside until the emergency has passed. This fact keeps us safe in many of life's threatening situations. It also sets up the possibility of addiction.

If our emotional center runs amuck and begins using its trumping ability, we can indulge in our drug of choice as an attempt—albeit dysfunctional—to try to meet and satisfy the needs within us. When our conditioning reaches the level of compulsion, we have compromised the system. It no longer functions as intended.

The emotional center now uses its trumping power to overcome our thinking brain, and exerts control over our lives. Our emotional center has hijacked the system. When we feel the activating emotion, we will act out, even if we do not want to. This manifests when the addict says, "I am not going to use, I am not going to use, I am not going to use," just before he uses. At this stage the emotional center is calling the shots and we have a compulsion and are well on our way to addiction.

Patrick Carnes, PhD, in his book, *Don't Call it Love*, presents the following description of the addictive process:

At some point, excessive use becomes compulsive use. The highs become so compelling that the person loses control. Usually the loss of control means serious consequences, yet the highs remain so compelling that the addict starts to distort, ignore or lose contact with reality. The addiction now regulates the emotional life of the addict. The addict cannot act "normal" without the high. Nor can the addict deal with stressors without the maladaptive response of the addiction. The inherent shamefulness of the addict brings on self destructive shame cycles, in which the addict's efforts to stop seem only to intensify the failures. The brain achieves a new neuro-chemical imbalance, which can only be relieved by compulsive use. The addict ends up isolated and alienated.

Once this point is reached, addicts cannot undo all the damage even with help. Significant shifts have occurred which leave them forever vulnerable to their addiction. Compulsive use always remains an option (Carnes 1992).

This is where others—"normies" who have never felt the power of compulsions—struggle to understand. "Why can't you just walk away?" they ask. In their lives, it has always worked. "If you keep drinking, you're going to lose your family—In heavens name, why can't you stop?" It seems so simple. Pretty cut and dry. When the addict can't walk away, judgments often are heaped on them.. "You must be really weak; don't you love your family? Why are you throwing your life away?"

Part of the struggle is a matter of intensity for the addict. Because of the conditioning process, urges for the normie might rate a 2.2 on the emotional Richter scale. To a normie, no big deal. For the addict, that same urge, after years of conditioning, feels like 7.5 plus. The compulsion is a major emotional event, (an emotional storm, if you will) and can not simply be ignored. An addict feels compelled to act and has little defense against it.

Coming Back: Discovery, Recovery, and Maintenance

Such is the state of addicts. Our emotional center is run amuck, hijacking our lives. We are out of control, acting out even when we are ashamed of our behaviors. How do we come back? How do we heal? How do we take back control of our lives?

It all begins with **Discovery**. Discovery refers to the process of realizing that we are, in fact, an addict; and, then, of coming to understand the devastating truth about what that truly means.

This is harder than it should be. Our denial and the addict inside of us like to get in the way. Addiction changes how we assimilate and process life's experiences. As addicts, we become very good at rationalization and justification and at denying that there is a problem.

It takes a while for us to come out of this fog of denial, to stop being blind to our addiction. The antidote of clarity comes in sobriety. We must establish and maintain sobriety, as it is the gateway to reality, helping us to understand who we have become, and what we are.

The Discovery Phase is also where we must turn to Jesus Christ, as He is our partner in recovery. *WE ARE SEEKING A CHANGE IN OUR HEART, A MIGHTY CHANGE. HE IS THE AUTHOR OF THAT CHANGE.* Some who suffer with addictions may have already known or been aware of Him, while some may be coming to Him for the first time; either way He is the true healer. True success and recovery requires that we establish conscious contact with Him, the Savior of us all.

We may feel unqualified, unworthy to be His follower. We may lack faith. Many have lost hope. But, these are the very feelings that can help us be humble and experience the beginnings of godly sorrow. President Ezra Taft Benson reminded us:

Godly sorrow is a gift of the Spirit. It is a deep realization that our actions have offense our Father and our God. It is the sharp and keen awareness that our behavior caused the Savior, He who knew no sin, even the greatest of all, to endure agony and suffering. Our sins caused Him to bleed at every pore. This very real mental and spiritual anguish is what the scriptures refer to as having "a broken heart and contrite spirit." Such a spirit is the absolute prerequisite for true repentance (Benson 1989).

Godly sorrow is one of those *absolute requirements* of recovery, but it often comes in stages throughout the journey. Don't worry if you do not feel an overwhelming sense of devotion or have an unwavering commitment right now. At this point, you may struggle to feel anything, except your urge to use—whjch you may feel deeply. This is not unusual as one of the hallmarks of addiction is a loss of connection with our emotions. Often, as addicts, we aren't able to connect consciously with our feelings. Time and behavioral changes will rectify that as we go on. Our commitment often appears in bits and pieces along the recovery highway; but, it will materialize, if we continue with honest effort, faith and sobriety.

The **Recovery Phase** is change making. We have come to a point of understanding how our behaviors have affected ourselves and others, and it is not a pretty picture. Through the doorway of godly sorrow, we develop the desire to make things right. Recovery is about making amends and remaking ourselves. It is about change and reinvention. It is about seeking...*to be reconciled to God;* for we know He is the source of our healing, *after all we can do* (2 Nephi 25:23).

The Recovery Phase is when we do all we can do. It necessitates doing our part of the work, putting in the needed effort. The required commitment overwhelms many. We still have life to live, jobs to maintain, family to care for, bills to pay, and responsibilities to meet. Remaking ourselves "on the fly" is not easy. The low success rates indicate how difficult a task it is.

In the Recovery Phase, addicts need to have two goals in mind. The first is to extinguish the bond that has been formed between our emotions or feelings and our drug of choice. The second goal we need to focus on during this phase is to find Christ and bring ourselves to Him. Both require sobriety and learning new life skills. To achieve these goals, Jeffrey R. Holland says: *We must change anything we can change that may be part of the problem* (Holland 2006).

The first goal, that of eliminating the existing bond between emotions and acting out, requires finding new, healthy ways to process difficult emotions. Over time, we *extinguish* the old bonds by establishing healthy new emotional bonds in their place. Healthy, is the key word here. Many addicts fall into the *cross-addiction* trap and merely find a new addictive response to their problematic emotions. Addicts also need to remember Carnes' warning: *Significant shifts have occurred ... Compulsive use always remains an option* (Carnes 1992). As addicts, we can always, easily, fall back into our addiction, even after years of sobriety.

The second goal of the Recovery Phase, finding Christ and bringing ourselves to Him, is about healing. It is our personal experience with Christ and our relationship to Him that is the source of the mending and healing we seek. Ultimately, our desire is to qualify for the words He spoke to the Nephites, when He said: *for I see that your faith is sufficient that I should heal you* (3 Nephi 17:8).

Elder Jeffery R. Holland teaches how we come to Christ:

The easiest and the earliest [step to Christ] comes simply with the desire of our heart, the most basic form of faith that we know. "If ye can no more than desire to believe," Alma says, exercising just "a particle of faith," giving even a small place for the promises of God to find a home—that is enough to begin...that simple step, when focused on the Lord Jesus Christ,...[is] the first step out of despair.

Second, we must change anything we can change that may be part of the problem. In short we must repent....We thank our Father in Heaven we are allowed to change, we thank Jesus we can change, and ultimately we do so only with Their divine assistance. Anything we can change we should change, and we must forgive the rest. In this way our access to the Savior's Atonement becomes as unimpeded as we, with our imperfections, can make it. He will take it from there.

Third, in as many ways as possible we try to take upon us His identity, and we begin by taking upon us His name. ... Above all else, loving with "the pure love of Christ," that gift that "never faileth," that gift that "beareth all things, believeth all things, hopeth all things, [and] endureth all things (Moroni 7:45-47). Soon, with that kind of love, we realize ... that every time we reach out, however feebly, for Him, we discover He has been anxiously trying to reach us (Holland, 2006).

The Recovery Phase is concerned with following the steps outlined by Elder Holland: find faith in Him, change everything we can that might be part of the problem, take His name upon ourselves, submit to His will and develop the pure love of Christ in our lives. That will put us in the Waters of Recovery that surround the Savior.

The benchmark which helps us know we are succeeding and that our recovery is happening, is when, after sustained sobriety, we can establish and maintain what we come to know as *serenity*. Serenity is that sweet, calming influence, that gentle, kind spirit, that profound feeling of peace and comfort, the knowledge that all is well, the very feeling of the pure love of Christ, directed by Him to us.

Maintenance Phase is about living a new way, or as Portia Nelson calls it, *Walking Down a Different Street* (Nelson 1994). As with each phase of this process, the Maintenance Phase requires that we develop new and different skills that help us maintain and protect what we have gained. We maintain our sobriety and serenity and continue our adventure of coming to Christ. We know the Maintenance is working when we feel the mighty change of heart stirring within us.

The ultimate goal of recovery is to feel the healing love of the Savior and discovering who we really are. That is how we come back. It is what Dr. Brown described as finding the lost self—A SELF LOST not only to ourselves, but also estranged from our family and our God. COMING BACK, RECOVERING, THEN IS THE FINDING OF WHAT HAS BEEN LOST.

When Hope is Lost

When we are trapped by our addiction or compulsions, we are sent into a proverbial tailspin. We begin losing things. Things like self respect, self worth and self love are early casualties. We don't even understand ourselves. We are often angered by our behaviors and our seeming lack of moral strength. Often we see ourselves as if we were two people, the good and worthwhile Dr. Jekyll and the out of control, despicable, destructive Mr. Hyde. We develop a disgust for ourselves. We become very judgmental. We may mount effort after effort to stop and to change our behavior(s), with seemingly no success. We always fail. We lose hope.

This is the dark place. The dismal, dreadful existence devoid of hope defies accurate description. We feel only despair. As our situation progresses, we feel things slipping away. One of the strengths of our faith is the quiet confidence we have in the Plan of Happiness (Alma 42:8). We know that in following a righteous life, there is a reuniting of loved ones and a joyful reunion with our Father and the Savior. For many Latter-day Saints, that understanding brings peace and comfort to every day. This, however, is not the case for the addict. He has lost hope for that. He has made too many mistakes. As he continues his behaviors, which are so contrary to the commandments, he realizes he is in a state in which he will not pass judgment, because he is unworthy. The promised blessings no longer apply for him. Though it is in a court of his own self-judgment he believes his peace, his confidence, his comfort are deemed forfeited, and he is left feeling very alone and condemned.

Somewhere in this process, shame sets in. Shame is that feeling that comes from an inner decision that there is *something wrong with me.* The scriptures say, *Be ye therefore perfect, even as your Father in Heaven is perfect* (Matt. 5:48). We live in a society of very good, moral, righteous people, but, as addicts, we don't see ourselves measuring up. "I mean, everybody else seems to not have a problem with this..." We harshly judge ourselves. We believe we have come up short. We are not worthy. We are not good enough. We are a piece of garbage and even worse. We bombard ourselves with hateful self-talk statements and thoughts, all of which have a toxic effect on us. Our motivation becomes challenged. Our will is compromised. Our view of life, the world and our place in it has changed significantly, and we feel there is very, very little that we can do to change things.

This loss of hope sometimes presents some startling features in addicts, especially those who are members of the Church of Jesus Christ of Latter-day Saints. Often LDS addicts come to recovery with parts of their faith intact. They know that God lives. They know that the gospel is true and that Joseph Smith was a prophet. They know the Savior died for all humankind, well sort of.

Members of the Church who struggle with addictions often become convinced that the healing power of the atonement can apply to all the rest of the world, but somehow the atonement excludes them. *I have done too much. I am unworthy. My sins are just too gross.* This kind of thinking is the manifestation of the loss of hope, which may also sound like this: *Healing is available, but not for me. I am defiled and have forfeited my rights to the blessings. It no longer applies to me.* Their life takes on an underlying sense of despair and is reduced to going through the motions.

The loss of hope is a paralyzing condition. When we see no possibility of success, we feel no motivation or strength to try. We become helpless and feel compelled to our fate; we are reconciled to being addicts. Can you imagine how Satan must feel at such a turn of events? His work is done. He can turn his attention elsewhere without much concern that there will be change. The addict is locked up by his own loss of hope, imprisoned without bars, but absolutely unable to progress or heal.

In Search of Healing

As Latter-day Saints, we are seen as a self-reliant people—extremely self-reliant people. We have a heritage of accomplishment and pride that sometimes gets in our way of accepting help from others and from the Lord. We take care of ourselves. We take care of our families. We have always been able to find our own solutions. It is the Mormon way. However, when we find ourselves in the grip of addiction and our solutions unsuccessful, we are at a loss. Reaching out is not natural to us. It feels uncomfortable, and it has most likely never been necessary before. The result is, we often struggle to seek or accept the help of others.

The problem is, addiction is not a maze that can be escaped from without the help of others. We need their guidance. As Elder Robert D. Hales said: *We must be self-sufficient ourselves, but that does not mean independent of help from others ... The disposition to ask assistance from others with confidence and to grant it with kindness, should be part of our very nature* (Hales, 1977).

Our bishop's wife once confessed to struggling with feelings that she was not a good mother. Of course, as the congregation listened, we reacted with disbelief. We all felt that she was an incredible mother, not only to her family but also in her role as the mother of our ward. She went on to teach how important it is for us to bear one another's burdens and to find the strength for our own struggle in the process of helping others in their challenges. Our bishop's wife seemed to understand and certainly exemplified that one of the requirements for this healing process to take place is that we must be willing to share our burdens. We must not hide our own struggles. We cannot help bear the burdens of others while we keep our own dark secrets. We must find the humility to allow others to help us, most especially in recovery. We cannot heal alone. The healing process requires the loving help of others and our submission to their assistance.

One of the features of working the Twelve Steps established by Alcoholics Anonymous and now used by other addiction recovery groups is that we become reliant on our Heavenly Father and his Son. They are the actual source of our healing, gifting us with the mighty change of heart of which Alma spoke (Alma 5:12, 14).

In *The Addiction Recovery Program* developed by the Church, we read in Step 3: *Decide to turn your will and your life over to the care of God the Eternal Father and His Son, Jesus Christ* (LDS Family Services, 2005). That is not a statement of reliance on self. That is a statement of total reliance on Him.

Unfortunately, these lines often get blurry for us. We thrive on the *Can Do!* spirit and on our enthusiasm for getting things done, often forgetting that we are totally reliant on Him. Maybe it is our human part wanting credit or taking pride, but it is a huge stumbling block for many. Unable to accept help, they cannot find the path out of their addictive behaviors.

And, Oh My! The lengths we go to avoid the embarrassment of others knowing. In many cases, it seems we would forgo getting help, if we thought someone would find out about our doing so. Individuals who have been invited to attend the Church's *Addiction Recovery Program*, don't typically ask questions like: "What do they do there?" Or, "How can it help me?" Instead, most often, they want to know: "Who will see me there?" Or "Who will know that I have this problem?"

Ron tells the story of when he lost his membership in the Church because of his acting out. It was years ago, when it was the practice of the Church to announce in priesthood meeting any excommunications that resulted from Church courts:

> *The bishop asked if I wanted to be somewhere else when he made the announcement of the results of my upcoming Church court. Anticipating that I was going to be excommunicated, I felt fairly certain that this would indeed be an embarrassing situation and I told him I would skip opening exercises. My court was the morning of that priesthood meeting and was a truly amazing spiritual experience. While I did lose my membership in the Church, I also felt in a very profound way that Heavenly Father loved me and that this was exactly the step that needed to take place for me to heal. That knowledge allowed me to forget about being embarrassed. This is what I needed to do. I welcomed it and became unconcerned about what others thought. I attended the meeting, sat through the announcement, but felt no embarrassment or shame, only the loving compassionate support of my friends and brothers.*

Ron found humility, which leads to recovery. Humility helps us avoid the fear of which people will know. It dismisses the harmful pride that would keep us from healing. It is a gateway to the path of recovery, a path that is often hidden from our view until we look with our eyes of faith and humility.

According to President Dieter F. Uchtdorf:

There are some who believe that because they have made mistakes, they can no longer fully partake of the blessings of the gospel. How little they understand the purposes of the Lord. One of the great blessings of living the gospel is that it refines us and helps us learn from our mistakes. We "all have sinned, and come short of the glory of God;" yet, the Atonement of Jesus Christ has the power to make us whole when we repent.

President Uchtdorf goes on to quote Elder Joseph B. Wirthlin who, he said, gave greater clarity to this issue when he said:

Oh, it is wonderful to know that our Heavenly Father loves us—even with all our flaws! His love is such that even should we give up on ourselves, He never will.

We [might] see ourselves in terms of yesterday and today. Our Heavenly Father sees us in terms of forever...

President Uchtdorf concludes:

The gospel of Jesus Christ is a gospel of transformation. It takes us as men and women of the earth and refines us into men and women for the eternities.

To those who have left the path of discipleship for whatever reason, I invite you to start where you are and come to the restored gospel of Jesus Christ. Walk again in the way of the Lord. I testify that the Lord will bless your life, endow you with knowledge and joy beyond comprehension, and distill upon you the supernal gifts of the Spirit. It is always the right time to walk in His way. It is never too late (Uchtdorf, 2009).

The remaining chapters of this book will outline many suggestions about how to leave addiction and live a happy, healthy, successful life. Many of the suggestions may not seem very spiritual in nature. All of them do, however, have spiritual implications. All are designed to help bring our attitudes and behaviors in line with the Savior's commandments and to qualify us for His healing touch. We are a bit like the woman of the Bible with an issue of blood ... like her, we are setting out to find where He is with the goal of getting close enough to Him that we may touch Him and be healed (Luke 8:43, 44).

The Dysfunctional Relationship: Addiction

Some clinicians use a model of treatment that considers addiction as a relationship replacement. Forming an addiction is often an effort to replace the benefits that human relationships were intended to give us, which we feel are missing in our lives. Brown declares, *the addiction becomes best friend, lover* (Brown, 2006).

We try to harvest from our addiction the nurturing and comfort that should come from developing and maintaining healthy relationships. It is a fool's quest. Our partner in the contrived relationship is not true to us, and becomes, as Brown describes, *The demon that will destroy the addict* (Brown, 2006). Even when we realize that it is a very dysfunctional relationship, that we are in bed with a demon, we are afraid to let go.

It stands to reason that part of the recovery process is establishing healthy relationships. It often requires some repair work to rebuild relationships that have been damaged, where hurt has been done, where trust is lost. In AA jargon, we must make *amends* and try to heal the damage we have caused. Recovery, and especially maintenance of that recovery, also involves integrity in forming new relationships, not taking advantage of others, being honest and trustworthy, as well as giving of ourselves. For some of us, this is a very new experience. We have never really known or had a relationship that could be described as healthy.

How Change Happens

Establishing sobriety is the beginning point of recovery. It is Mile 0 on the Recovery Highway. Sobriety eases the power of our addictive-thinking errors. We begin to see things quite differently from the vantage point of sobriety. For individuals in Washington state's DUI Diversion Program, combining time with sobriety makes for some amazing changes in attitude. The typical client entering the program's intensive outpatient segment is quite sure he does not have a problem, and he often rails against the system and the injustice of his situation. Clients in the last months of the program, after two years of treatment and sobriety, talk about new clarity and personal success in their lives. Many, in the end, view their arrest as a blessing.

Abstinence from our drug of choice is not the same as recovery. Establishing abstinence is an event. Recovery is the long-term developmental process that follows that event. Abstinence means we are achieving sobriety, and we are not using our drug of choice. The process of recovery is ongoing healing, or moving away from denial, deceptions, and self gratifications. It is making steps toward a life of honesty, truly loving and being loved, serving others and learning to live in the Waters of Recovery.

There has been a common belief perpetuated that we must hit bottom before recovery can begin and that, somehow, each addict must wallow in the resultant mire of his addictive behaviors before he can change his life. It is believed that an appropriate amount of suffering must occur before change can happen. However, we know now that through clinical intervention we can *raise the bottom.*

Addiction is accompanied by a web of thinking errors and denial. Twelve steppers call it *Stinkin' Thinkin'.* The readiness for recovery is determined more by the stopping of stinkin' thinkin' than by bouncing on our "rock" bottom and the accomplishment of suffering. While the suffering can clear the denial and bring back reality (often at a horrific price), the same thing can be accomplished with clinical intervention.

If an addict can be helped in confronting his thinking errors, he can raise his bottom and progress through what Miller refers to as a series of stages of change (Miller, 2002).

Understanding this process is helpful in recognizing where the addict is in terms of changing behavior. It is the "teaching the pigs to sing" concept. If the addict is not in the appropriate stage of change, don't hold the expectation that wonderful songs are about to be sung. They will not be. The addict is not ready to learn to sing. Holding singing lessons at this point won't do much good.

If we can meet the addict where he is, in whatever stage that might be, and clinically help move him to the next step, and then the next, recovery can occur. Before you know it, he is ready for lessons—and you just might hear a beautiful chorus. Recognizing the stage of change tells us what the addict needs next in the process of healing.

An addict who has no interest in even thinking about changing would be said to be in *pre-contemplation stage* of change. His conversation may sound like this:

My life is fine. There are no problems with my substance use or anything else. Or. he might also say: *At times, I have noticed things get out of hand for me; some people have said some things, but I am not worried and don't see any need to change.* The addict isn't in much danger of healing in this stage.

He might move to *contemplation stage,* when the thought of changing enters his mind but he is not really entertaining any ideas about how change would occur. This would be the stage where the addict would ask himself if he should stop using or acting out. He may say something like this:

Part of me thinks I would like to see if I could cut down on using, and another part of me thinks I am fine. Or, his conversation could sound like this: *When others tell me I need to change, I find myself telling them why I can't or that now is not a good time...sometimes I think I should change, but...*

When the addict starts thinking about what change might be like or how that might occur, he has reached the *preparation stage.* What he says may sound like this:

I have made up my mind to quit using, but I am not sure how to do that.

Or, perhaps, like this: *I know I can change, but I need more information on how to meet my goals.*

With additional help, he then might be ready to enter the stage of *action,* where he begins making changes in his life. His speaking will then sound like this:

I am making changes and having some success!

Or, this: *Sometimes this isn't easy, but I am feeling more confident all the time.*

Maintenance is the last stage of change. It is the process of keeping the changes in place in our lives. The maintenance voice will sound like this:

I am committed to maintaining what I have changed. Or *Even if I slip or relapse, I intend to keep working on maintaining the changes I have made* (Tomlin, 2004).

With the appropriate clinical intervention, a client might move though these stages rather quickly. Without help, addicts can oscillate between pre-contemplation and contemplation for some time, not changing anything, but remaining lost in their addictions until the harsh realities of hitting a bottom and their suffering bring them to action. Or, they may embrace their suffering and self destruction, becoming lost forever to their demon.

For those of us that are seeking addiction recovery, it is helpful to understand that there is a way we can gauge our own place in relationship to change. We can tell where we are by listening to our language. If we find ourselves, saying our lives are fine and there is no reason to change, we are not going to be doing much healing any time soon.

It's true that there are certain individuals who experience the process of *natural recovery*. Shane is an example. He says:

> *I was a pot smoker from the time I was 14 until I was 28. I thought I would never stop smoking. Why should I? I really liked the way it calmed down my ADHD symptoms and mellowed me out. I got through college smoking pretty much every day and got a decent job without having to stop. Even when I got married, it was no big deal. My wife smoked some and didn't make a big deal of my use. Four years later, we had a little baby girl. She is amazing. I didn't think much about it while my wife was pregnant but, at the birth, when they put that beautiful, precious little girl in my arms, I knew that I was done smoking. I haven't smoked since.*

Shane had outlived his addiction's usefulness. He realized that the birth of his daughter and his commitment to her far outweighed the benefits of his daily bowl of marijuana. The truth is, however, not all addicts react as Shane did. Not all find that healing moment in their lives. We cannot wait for the blessed magical arrival of natural recovery to deliver us from addiction. We must be proactive and search for answers. We must engage in the work of recovery.

How Did I Get to the Falls?

> *"Ron, you do realize you are a sexual addict don't you?"*
> *he said with some frustration in his tone.*
>
> *I was stunned and dumfounded. I couldn't find the*
> *words for a reply.*
>
> *"No, actually I did not realize that," I finally muttered.*
> *In fact, I was sure I wasn't anything like a sex addict.*
>
> *Up to this moment, I had really liked this therapist.*
> *I trusted him, how could he suggest such a thing? I had*
> *found his wisdom and insights very helpful as I worked*
> *through my recovery from my emotionally abusive child-*
> *hood and depression issues. He always had the ability to*
> *cut to the heart of the matter, but had his clinical judgment*
> *suddenly left him?*
>
> *I was NOT a sex addict. I was NOT that guy!*
>
> *Yes, I had some problems with affairs in my adult life;*
> *there were some things I wasn't too proud of, but an addict,*
> *and a sexual addict to boot, NO WAY!*
>
> *He didn't argue with me. He just gave me a copy of*
> *"The White Book" published by Sexaholics Anonymous*
> *and told me to read it. By page 38, I was convicted.*
>
> *So, there I was, overwhelmed, with the newfound*
> *knowledge that I was a sex addict. Now what? How did I*
> *ever get to this spot?*

It is said there are only seven scripts in Hollywood, that each new movie is just a retelling of a familiar story line. How many times have we seen *Romeo and Juliet* set in a new period with characters bearing new names, but still conveying the same tragic story? Like scripts, there are only a few well-traveled roads that lead to addiction.

Finding the road that brought us to the precipice of the falls can give us direction in moving to the Waters of Recovery. While it is true that many of the rules of recovery must be observed by all addicts, every person in recovery faces some unique elements, elements that hold clues to healing their own particular underlying issues. A competent clinician would not treat someone who had become addicted to pain pills while recovering from surgery with the same treatment plan as an individual medicating the pain of childhood trauma, or as someone who drinks in excess because of being raised in a family culture of alcohol abuse.

Exploring the history of the addiction and finding the underlying issues are paramount to building recovery and relapse prevention plans and maintaining sobriety. Underlying issues act as the powerful, invisible undertows on the river to the waterfalls. The issues lying beyond our awareness can dictate the addict's direction of travel.

> *John was a recovering sex addict who started attending Sexaholic Anonymous meetings as part of his recovery plan. All of this Twelve-Step stuff was new to him, but he had made a decision that if these folks had some ideas that would help him, he would follow their direction. John was also a survivor of childhood sexual abuse, which was one of his underlying addiction issues. He had spent nearly two years in therapy working on recovery from those tragic events. This work had been completed before he even realized he was also a sexual addict. John took to the meetings and the fellowship, found a sponsor and progressed nicely in his sobriety and recovery.*
>
> *John also found a new friend. His name was Ernie and John described him as a "John Clone." They felt an instant bond. They were nearly the same age and their lives had traveled an eerily common path. They had been sexually abused in a similar manner when they were the same age. Their form of acting out was identical, and they had suffered very similar consequences from their addictions. John noticed that Ernie, like himself, appeared to be very sincere and diligent in working his program. What he also noticed was that Ernie was not able to maintain sobriety*

and make strides in recovery. It was puzzling to John that if they were both sincerely working towards, and desiring recovery, why it was eluding his friend.

Then, one evening at group, as John was listening intently to Ernie, he realized that the issue Ernie was talking about and struggling with was really an underlying sex abuse issue, and not an addiction recovery issue. Because John had spent two years working on the childhood sex abuse issues, he was now free to work on addiction recovery. Ernie did not have that luxury. His sex abuse issues kept rising up and sabotaging his recovery efforts. John pulled Ernie aside and mentioned his observations and helped Ernie find a good therapist to help quiet his underlying issues. It wasn't long before Ernie, too, was building sobriety and establishing recovery.

As the story of Ernie suggests, this is the point at which the benefits of individual therapy may be of great help to the recovery process, but finding an appropriate therapist can sometimes be challenging. It is critical that they understand and have worked with other addicts. Equally important, for therapists working with addicts who are Mormons. is an understanding what being a member of the Church means. Moreover, to effectively help individuals struggling with addictions a therapist must be able to connect on a level that will allow you to reveal intimate, difficult and personal material. Cinical exploration of issues detrimental to the client's healing can free him to move upstream to recovery. It has the effect of pulling up the anchor that has held the addict in his addiction.

Some Roads to the Waterfalls:
Childhood Sexual Abuse/Trauma /Abandonment

Survivors of childhood, physical, emotional or sexual abuse, as well as victims of traumatic events, and children who have been abandoned (by parents who are not present physically or are absent emotionally), often resort to medicating their pain through addiction. They find comfort from the emotional pain in their lives. It begins as a coping strategy, which, through the conditioning process, becomes compulsion and addiction.

There is something missing in their emotional development. Their emotional foundation was never completed and they struggle to function. We have great difficulty meeting our needs without that foundation. Abraham Maslow suggested this foundation is built from knowing that we will survive the day and that we are safe in the world. These children never had the comfort of knowing they were safe. Without establishing this basic need, our other needs become very, very difficult to meet and our emotional dysfunction gets in the way.

This is a simplified version of Maslow's view of our basic human needs:

1.   Survival—Having food and shelter to survive.

2.   Safety—Freedom from danger, safe and secure in the world.

3.   Loving and Being Loved

4.   Accomplishment—Contributing in a meaningful way.

5.   Being the Best We Can Be (Maslow 1962)

When, for example, safety is compromised by sexual abuse or trauma, the ability to meet the need to love and be loved, and all other needs above that, are compromised. We struggle to love and be loved because we might suffer terrible jealousy or be so controlling (trying to be safe) that no one can stand to live with us. The emotional pain generated by such experience begs to be soothed. The self-nurturing relief of addiction seems to be the perfect solution, in the beginning.

> *Andy suffered from abandonment issues as a result of his drug-addicted mother. She was physically present, but unable to care for him or be available for him emotionally when she was lost in her addiction. Andy's aunt told him of a time when he was two, when she observed him dressed only in a messy diaper, crying and reaching up to his mother for her care and comfort. His mother pushed him aside because she was busy using and getting ready to shoot up with heroin. It was a symbolic moment of his childhood.*

> *Andy is now 21 and very interested in having a girl-friend, but reports that his relationships never last more than a month or two. Andy is a heavy pot smoker. He is also decent looking and has a great sense of humor. He has some very dysfunctional relationship behaviors. He really wants to feel loved, but he comes off as very controlling. (He is still worrying about the possibility of more abandonment like he felt from his mother.) He feels a strong need to know everyone that his girlfriend has contact with. If they go to a party, Andy cannot allow his girlfriend to be in a separate room because he is afraid she might meet someone else and leave with them. After a few weeks, even though Andy has a lot going for him, his girlfriends break off the relationship because they feel smothered by him. Andy turns to his bong for comfort, but it is never enough.*

Andy is desperately trying to love and be loved, but he has never been able to establish that it is safe in this world or that he is loved and wanted. No one was ever there to confirm that for him. Without establishing safety, he struggles at meeting his need to love and be loved. Now his addiction and neediness (his fear of further loss) get in the way, the controlling behavior drives away any potential girlfriends. The addiction certainly isn't meeting his needs either, although he feels better when he is high. Hence, the sentence for practicing dysfunctional ways is that we are forever trying to meet our needs in ways that can never meet our needs.

Shame-Based Personalities

These are also medicators.

> *Ruth refers to the things that she is avoiding through her sexual addiction as "the sadness." It presents in her as a very profound sense of rejection, disappointment and shame. She*

states, "I just feel like I am not who I should be." She first be-came aware of the feeling when, after singing a song at church with her Primary class, she returned to her seat, feeling very proud and hoping she had pleased her parents. When her fa-ther asked why she hadn't smiled, the comment cut through her to the core. She hadn't done it right. She didn't act the way she was supposed to, even though she had tried very, very hard.

As an attractive, bright, 36-year-old, she still bore the sadness and shame and only found relief in the euphoria associated with falling in love. Relationship after relation-ship would mask the pain, but not heal it. She went from partner to partner, in a constant state of falling in love, without ever quieting the sadness or feeling worthy.

When Ruth began to heal her shame and to realize she was exactly who she was supposed to be, she didn't need medication any longer and the need to engage in her addiction diminished. Real changes started happening in her life. Addictive behaviors have less hold on us when underlying issues are resolved.

Some may have been tempted to treat Ruth by teaching her how to set boundaries, such as how to make better choices or advancing her relationship skills. We like trying to treat symptoms, even though it is always better to treat causes. Ruth's need to act out disappeared when she worked through her shame and learned she was exactly who she was supposed to be, and she was, by anyone's standard, a very special person.

Early Sexualization

Children exposed to sexual content before maturation are susceptible to the lure of sexual addictions.

Peter was raised by what he describes as "hippie" parents. He has vivid memories of drug and alcohol use from his very earliest memories. He was allowed to begin using marijuana and LSD at the age of 5. His parents and friends often had sex in areas where he could observe them, and he began re-enacting the sexual activities he witnessed with his younger sister when he was 10. At age 41, he came to my office, struggling to kick a nasty alcohol addiction. He could consume legendary amounts of alcohol and still maintain a semblance of function. He was surprised to find out that having had upwards of 65 sexual partners might mean he also had a sexual addiction.

By nature of our sexually explicit culture, early sexualization is increasingly affecting our children. It is like trying to run our 220-volt dryer with wires that were designed for charging our cell phone. The wiring is just too delicate to handle the tremendous voltage. Young developing minds are likewise incapable of handling the highly charged sexually explicit material that seems available at every turn. It destroys normal development and creates a dysfunctional decision-making system around sexual issues.

Biological/Cultural Predisposition

A percentage of our population have the inborn, genetic predisposition to addiction or are raised in an addiction culture. Experience with addictive behaviors makes sense to these individuals and has a compulsion that those outside of the percentile group do not feel.

In his book on sex addiction, called *Don't Call it Love*, Patrick Carnes, PhD, describes the cultural aspect of predisposition: *Certain children are especially susceptible to the addiction process. These children live in our addiction-prone culture. They probably have parents who are addicted to one or more behaviors or substances ... most often the children are abused, probably in several ways. These children are the vulnerable children.*

...They seek to feel better. They are not bad children, but rather children in pain who seek relief. They will use "highs" to feel better—food, sex, TV— whatever numbs the pain... (Carnes, 1992).

Being hardwired for addiction has an inevitable ring to it. However, it's important to understand that predisposition is a tendency, not a sentence. Those with predisposition, who learn healthy emotional skills, need not suffer an inevitable curse, even though they do have a susceptibility that the general population does not have. It is an issue that normies struggle to understand. Normies might wonder why these individuals just don't say no; to normies, it seems as simple as a choice. The reality is that predisposed individuals are dealing with some dynamics that are not felt or understood by normies.

> Ann was a 36-year-old mother, who was struggling with a serious meth addiction. She had dabbled in several drugs and used alcohol all of her life, but it was always on a take-it-or-leave-it basis. She used frequently, but could always walk away, and she never lost control or fell into excess. In her earlier years, she was judgmental of some of her friends who had serious drug problems.
>
> Then she met Tommy. Tommy mainlined meth, which at the time was a fairly new drug craze. With her open approach to drug use, Ann accepted Tommy's invitation to shoot up with him. Ann's description of what happened next really tells the story. "I fell in love! I used daily for the next three weeks until I crashed [in exhaustion]. When I woke up four days later, I couldn't wait to get a needle and go again."

Ann found a drug that triggered her predisposition, a high that was compelling beyond anything she had felt before. That is the problem for people with biological or cultural predisposition; sometimes the bus leaves the station without warning.

> Millie really didn't have a drug or alcohol problem until she was in her mid-30s. Millie was raised in a family with a significant alcohol and drug abuse history. Millie, however, had managed to dodge the addiction bullet. She

had always been successful in her work, college educated, and enjoyed many friends. When her husband of 12 years left her and their son very unexpectedly, she was devastated. She began to drink for comfort, and, in a very short time, was drinking for the sake of drinking.

What had held no interest for her earlier in her life now became Millie's demon. Her predisposition came into play when it was combined with the devastation she felt from the sudden abandonment by her husband.

Recreational User Who Got Off Trail

These are experimenters and recreational users that fall prey to their own conditioning behaviors. These are like Pinocchio when he went to the fair and, at the end of the day realized,—much to his surprise,—that he wasn't a little boy anymore.

If we think of addiction in a linear way, beginning with recreational or experimental use that progresses to compulsive use and then to addictive use, we can begin to understand these addicts. It is really about conditioning, about the forming of a bond between difficult emotions and a drug of choice. This is the same process that Pavlov demonstrated with his now-famous dogs. Pavlov noticed his dogs' mouths started to water when he brought them food. One day, he began to also ring a bell when he brought the food. After a time, he rang only the bell and the dog's mouths still watered.

They had become conditioned to react this way. The dogs had grown to establish a relationship between hearing the bell and mouth watering. Recreational users are conditioning themselves without being aware. Each time they use, the emotional center makes note that they don't feel anxiety (or any other difficult emotion) while using. With continued use, this realization grows into a strong emotional bond between our stressors and our drug of choice.

In the beginning, it might just be an occasional weekend social event, but, as the connection is made and reinforced that relief from

29

difficult feelings comes from our drug of choice, we make steady progress towards compulsion and addiction. When the emotional bond has been formed, the individual no longer waits for a social time to drink, because it has become about more than being social. The emotional center sends out a request for consumption whenever difficult feelings arise.

Soon a compulsive feature to the conditioning develops. Again, with compulsion, the individual's urge to drink is greater than his will to say no, and the addictive process really takes off. Eventually, full-blown addiction sets in, where the individual is drinking for no other reason than he needs alcohol in his body to function. That first drink in the morning steadies his hands and removes the pain from his body. It is not recreational or experimental any longer. It is dependence, a full-blown addiction.

Spiritual Replacement

For every individual, there is a certain loneliness about earth life. When it comes to our separation from Father, some feel it more acutely than others. For someone who has had little or no spiritual upbringing or influence, the comfort of indulgence in drugs and alcohol might ease the pain of not having spiritual connection. It fills a spiritual void. One alcoholic said of it: *I have been looking for something all my life. I don't yet know what it is. I will know it when I find it.* For many years, she thought that "something" was in the bottle. She now knows it is not. She is still looking.

Scott Peck has offered that addiction is a *disease of the soul, the ultimate loneliness* (Peck 1993). Our addiction further separates us from God. Because of the progressive nature of the disease, the separation increases as we stay in our addiction. Our new god is a very jealous god and is not interested in sharing us with anyone. We increase our isolation, becoming more devoted to our compulsions and losing ourselves more completely with each passing addictive day.

As we ponder our addiction's genealogy, it is worth noting that some of us have several of these predisposing elements present in our lives. There is no single underlying cause. We may have been raised in an alcohol culture and been physically abused, or we may have suffered the childhood death of a parent, or, perhaps we were exposed to pornography at an early age. Regardless, most addicts have more than one underlying cause. There is a message for the addict in finding the underlying issue(s). Finding that underlying cause helps make sense of an addiction and aids in the process of restoring hope. For the clinician, it gives direction to treatment.

Recovery in this area is two-pronged. The addict should work to resolve underlying issues, in order to diminish emotional effects. At the same time, the addict should develop new emotional management skills that increase both his tolerance and his ability to deal with emotional discomfort. Bringing down the emotional effects of underlying issues, along with raising the ability to tolerate emotional challenges, can bring the two into healthy manageable balance.

The Potential Gifts of Our Addiction

Bruce Hafen gave this perspective:

So if you have problems in your life, don't assume there is something wrong with you. Struggling with those problems is at the very core of life's purpose. As we draw close to God, He will show us our weaknesses and through them make us wiser, stronger. If you're seeing more of your weaknesses, that just might mean you're moving nearer to God, not farther away (Hafen, 2004).

When we realize that the purpose of life is not so much the process of being judged but rather the process of learning and growing, we can look with new eyes on our problems here. If we focus on life being about judgment, it doesn't take very long for us to make enough mistakes that we feel like we are going to fail this test. It can be discouraging. It almost feels like the test is rigged. We are very imperfect beings, who have been asked to *be ye therefore perfect* (Matt. 5: 48). Being perfect is not a reality of this lifetime for us. It just cannot be done.

If we look at this life in a different way, realizing that our purpose is learning and growing, our weaknesses make a lot more sense.

31

I give unto men weakness that they might be humble; and my grace is sufficient for all men that humble themselves before me; for if they humble themselves before me, and have faith in me, then will I make weak things become strong unto them (Ether 12:27).

If He gives unto us weakness, we may assume He is not going to be too surprised that we feel compelled to act out in that weakness. He is not going to be shocked to learn that we have become addicts. Now, that isn't said in a way that condones acting out or gives permission for getting lost in our addictions and sins, and it is not said to make the excuse, "God made me this way!" Rather, it is said to give perspective. We have been given weaknesses to bring us to God. Use it for that purpose. Allow it to humble you and help you get to God.

If we can follow the admonition He gave to humble ourselves before Him and have faith in Him, then we have the opportunity for Him to make this weak thing strong. In this way, our addiction has served a great purpose. Our suffering, and the suffering we have caused others, will not be in vain. However, we must act. We must bring ourselves to Him in humility.

The handcart pioneers came to know God in their extreme suffering. They counted it as a privilege to pay that price because of the gift they received of knowing Him (Hafen 2004).

In the Book of Mormon, when the poor were excluded from the synagogues, Alma suggested *it is well that ye are cast out of your synagogues, that ye might be humble* (Alma 32:12). Alma taught that it was a blessing to be compelled to be humble, because this sometimes causes us to seek repentance and find mercy from such compulsion (Alma 32:13). He also taught that it is better for us to find the humility to repent on our own, *yea,* [they who can humble themselves are] *much more blessed than they who are compelled to be humble* (Alma 32:15).

But Alma, like the addict seeking Christ, experienced his own way of being compelled to humility. His experience came not from a drug of choice or out of a bottle, but at the hands of an angel of God. For the handcart pioneers it was their extreme suffering. The important thing in all of this is that we humble ourselves before God and come to know Him.

The prodigal son also came to know Him in his suffering (Luke 15:11-32).

A certain man had two sons and the younger of them said, Father give me the portion of goods that falleth to me...And not many days after the younger son gathered all together and took his journey into a far country and there wasted his substance with riotous living.

Some might want to apply judgment upon the foolish prodigal son at this point, but, for him, the learning process is now beginning. With all his wealth spent, and finding himself in want, he becomes a feeder of swine to survive; *he would fain have filled his belly with the husks that the swine did eat: and no man gave unto him.* He had fallen about as far as a person could fall. The situation he found himself in, which was caused by his own imprudence, was degrading and embarrassing and created room for humility. *And when he came to himself,* he desired to be but a servant in his father's house.

This is the moment Heavenly Father waits for in each of us; the point when we come to ourselves and turn to Him in humility and faith. We really have no idea how long that process took for the prodigal son, how long he suffered in that situation, or the extent of the hardships that he endured. We only know that he was in a setting that allowed that blessed moment to occur, when he came to himself. In the eternal scheme of things, serving in the swine lot, was a great blessing to the prodigal.

Many of us also need such a setting. The prodigal son arose with only a desire to be a servant in his Father's house. He welcomed that prospect. He recognized what a blessing it was to hold that station. The purpose of life is that we all come to a similar realization. If our struggle brings us to Christ, if it brings us in humility and submission to Him, then it has been a blessing. If we must lose everything and feed swine to find that moment of understanding, then perhaps we should be asking where the swine are.

CHAPTER 2

Moving Upstream to Safety

Getting Started

*I*t is time to move upstream away from the waterfalls to safety and find the Waters of Recovery. It is time to leave the acting out of our addiction and break free of its control over us. It is time to establish sobriety.

The addict is quick to ask: *How do I stop doing what I can't stop doing? How do I change what I have been unable to change?*

The answer to that question is fairly simple, but the doing of it is not. If we judge by the number of people who fail, sobriety is difficult to accomplish. In order to stop doing what we can't stop doing, we will have to make many changes in the way we live and in the way we process life. Thoughts, attitudes, behaviors and beliefs are just a few of the things we must overhaul. Elder Holland directs: *We must change anything we can that may be part of the problem* (Holland 2006), but our ultimate recovery and healing simply begins and ends at the feet of the Savior.

Come unto Christ and be perfected in Him, and deny yourself of all ungodliness; love God with all your might, mind and strength, then is his grace sufficient for you, that by his grace ye may be perfect in Christ (Moroni 10:32).

Recovery is the process of stopping the acting out of our addiction and accessing the grace of Christ. Later in this chapter, the Rules of

35

Early Recovery will be presented. Following this section, there will be more rules to follow, new skills to build and recovery tools to obtain. These are all things we can do to find recovery and deny ourselves of all ungodliness. We are seeking the Lord and His healing powers by loving Him with all our might, mind and strength. Our addiction has denied our ability to access Him in the past, and our goal is that He will see our efforts and, as Nephi writes, *know that our faith is worthy of His healing power* (3 Nephi 17:8).

We are moving upstream to safe waters, where we can escape the power of our addiction. Those safe waters surround Him. As Moroni teaches: *He is the one that can make weak things strong. His grace is indeed sufficient for us* (Ether 12:27).

Moroni continues that if we *are perfect in Christ, then are ye sanctified in Christ...through the shedding of the blood of Christ,...unto the remission of your sins, that ye become holy without spot* (Moroni 10:33).

Accessing the power of the atonement, (the shedding of the blood of Christ) avails us the healing (or the remission of our sins) that we seek as we try to leave our addiction. We seek to become holy, without the spot of addiction.

What follows are guidelines and directions that help us accomplish this spiritual goal. There is much we must do, including the change of anything we are doing that might be contributing to the problem. Some of the suggestions and directions are very spiritual in nature. Some are not. Each is important and plays its part. All come together to orchestrate recovery.

The process of healing is like putting together a giant jigsaw puzzle, a puzzle for which we are not provided the pieces. We must seek and find them. That is the work of recovery. We gather them from many places and sources and, sometimes, these are quite unlikely sources. Our part is to present ourselves ready and willing to do the work.

The Four Attitudes of Recovery

Four attitudes are essential possessions for anyone seeking to successfully move upstream to the Waters of Recovery. These attitudes position us for, and foster, healing and enable us to sustain our effort. Very little can be accomplished without these attitudes of recovery. They are what can provide us with the resilience required to stay the course in battling against the pull of the falls. Recovery can be a very arduous and challenging process, and accomplishing our healing will take all that we have. These Attitudes of Recovery outfit us for giving our all.

The Attitudes of Recovery are: *Willingness, Commitment, Courage, and Accountability.*

Willingness: ... *willing to submit to all things which the Lord seeth fit to inflict upon him* (Mosiah 3:19). Willingness allows us to submit to the process and rigors of healing and recovery, the process of coming to Christ.

When we combine faith and humility, we create the blessings of willingness and the power of submission to the healing process.

We know that faith has its origins in a desire to believe something and having hope. Alma explains that *if ye have faith ye hope for things which are not seen, which are true* (Alma 32:21). He also tells us that even if we can only desire to believe, but can plant the seed of the word in our hearts, and nurture and tend to it properly, it will grow into faith (Alma 32:27-42). Faith allows us to move forward, even though we may not be sure where the recovery process may take us.

The LDS Bible Dictionary states: *To have faith is to have confidence in something or someone.* We need confidence in the healing process provided (the something), and also confidence in Him who provided it (the someone).

In the language of the Twelve Steps, we say that we *are powerless* [of ourselves] *to overcome our addictions* and that our *lives have become unmanageable*; but *we have come to believe that the power of God can restore us to complete spiritual health* (LDS Family Services, 2004).

Humility is the catalyst for all learning, especially spiritual things (Oaks, 1994). Catalyst is a great descriptor for humility, because when we bring humility into our recipe or equation for healing, things really start to happen.

What makes humility such a powerful catalyst is that many things are not present once we are able to establish a position of humility.

Pride, arrogance, selfishness and self will are toxic to healing, but they cannot coexist and be present with humility. Without the destructive influence of these toxic behaviors, recovery is stimulated and given a place. When pride and its associates are replaced with humility, a willingness to be taught, an openness, a desire to comply, and a sensitivity to the spirit and its messages emerges. Obedience becomes important, and a spirit of cooperation develops within the addict, which displaces the spirit of contention and pridefulness.

One of the evidences that healing is taking place is the absence of contention. Contention cannot rear its head in a willing, submissive heart. If we find that contention is still present in our behaviors, we can know that we have not yet developed the Attitude of Willingness necessary for healing.

When the sum of our faith and humility is sufficient, it reaches a type of spiritual critical mass. Hope is then fostered and grows; a willing heart emerges, which generates the ability for us to be submissive. We truly become willing to submit to all things. When we have gained the ability to submit, the Lord's blessings become available to us. We can access His healing powers. They can be found in no other way.

As we move forward and take stock of our progress in recovery, two benchmarks that we will be looking for are *the return of hope* and the *willingness to do the work*. When these two things appear and are evident, it indicates the Attitude of Willingness has been attained.

Commitment: We must make a commitment to do the work of recovery. We must do whatever is necessary, no matter what tempts us to do otherwise. Make no mistake, this race isn't the 100 meters or even the mile, this is more like the *Iron Man Triathlon*. There will be times when you feel like you can't go on or like you are making no progress. Other times, you just like the idea of acting out. As one addict put it: *There were times when I just wanted to act out. My heart was set on it.* Those are the days when we come to understand that there is a work involved in recovery. Stated another way, there is struggle in recovery.

There are reasons for your commitment to be made now, for as the rush of hours, days and months grows stronger, the will to commit grows weaker.

The winds of tribulation ... blow out some men's candles of commitment (Maxwell 1974). To find healing and recovery, we must not allow that to happen. Our struggles and tribulation cannot blow out our candle of commitment. We must nurture, defend and protect our candle and keep it out of the fierce winds that are created by the denial and thinking errors of our addiction. We must remember that time is against us. If we put off our commitment, *the will ... grows weaker.*

Ron tells of his adventure:

> *As I flew across Alaska with a newly hired crew of construction workers, I listened to their stories and dreams. We were being paid well and had been promised almost unlimited overtime. We were all caught up in dreams of what might be. One was going to buy a new 18-wheeler with his earnings, another was to put a down payment on a fishing lodge, and yet another was to use the hoped-for money to start his own construction company. We were all intoxicated with the thoughts of the thousands of dollars we could earn on this job.*
>
> *Then our plane landed.*
>
> *The airport (if it could be called that) was the frozen ice of the Bering Sea. It was well below freezing, and winds blew at speeds of 40 miles per hour. Snow and ice covered everything. A board left on the ground during the lunch break would disappear in a snow drift. The conditions were horrendous. The layers and layers of clothes that we had to wear to stay warm made the simplest movements and tasks difficult. Working 8 hours a day was very tiring and the challenge of working 12 or 14 hours was impossible to all but one or two of us. The adversity we found in these difficult conditions quickly ended the financial dreams of most of our crew. The reality of our conditions was just too harsh for some dreams to endure.*

Out went their candles of commitment.

The Savior's teachings about commitment include: *He that shall endure to the end, the same shall be saved* (Matt. 24:13), and, also, *If ye continue in my word, then are ye my disciples indeed* (John 8:31). Nephi suggested that we *press forward with a steadfastness in Christ. Having a perfect brightness of hope, and love of God and of all men. Wherefore. if ye shall press forward feasting upon the word of Christ, and endure to the end, behold, thus saith the Father: Ye shall have eternal life* (2 Nephi 31:20).

Elder Joseph Wirthlin asked: *May I suggest three attributes to foster endurance in our day?*

First, testimony. Testimony gives us the eternal perspective necessary to see past the trials or challenges we will inevitably face. Second, humility. Humility is the recognition and attitude that one must rely on the Lord's assistance to make it through this life. We cannot endure to the end on our own strength. Without Him, we are nothing (John 15:5). *Third, repentance. The glorious gift of repentance allows us to return to the path with a new heart* (Wirthlin, 2004).

Elder Wirthlin has it right. Keeping our perspective (and having the eternal perspective) allows us to experience our challenges without being derailed by them. We know they are just challenges. Humility is the stance that allows the spirit to act upon us. It is ever vital. Repentance is what we need to return to the path, and what an important part of healing it is. Repentance allows us to be steadfast. It allows us to renew our efforts over and over, as many times as we need, to make our way to Him and healing.

Recovery has its own harsh realities. **Courage** is one of the tools we must grasp and add to our personal toolbox in order to protect our candle of commitment. Mother Theresa suggested *to have courage for whatever comes in life—everything lies in that* (McCain, 2004). Indeed, especially for our labor of recovery, everything does lie in, or depend on, our moral courage. We will be working in extreme emotional conditions. We have to face and overcome our greatest weaknesses and fears. We will have to vanquish our inner demons. Tremendous emotional storms will erupt. Our addictions do not want to die. They will give us a tremendous battle. For many, it is the greatest struggle of their lives. Many fail. To avoid that fate, make your resolve sure by protecting and nurturing your candle of commitment with Courage.

When Moses was taken from the Children of Israel, and the mantle of leadership fell to Joshua, the Lord spoke to him about the need for courage: *Be strong and of a good courage: for unto this people shalt thou divide for an inheritance the land. Only be thou strong and very courageous, that thou mayest observe to do according to all the law ... that thou mayest prosper whithersoever thou goest ... Be strong and of a good courage; be not afraid, neither be thou dismayed: for the Lord thy God is with thee whither-soever thou goest* (Joshua 1:7-9).

Obviously the Lord knew Joshua would need courage to accomplish what he was asked. He needed courage to divide the land, courage to keep the law, and courage to be neither afraid or dismayed. We all understand the fears of life—fear of the unknown, fear of our peers, fear of our self nature, fear of failure and even fear of success. We come to be dismayed in a number of ways: anger, frustration, disappointment, discouragement and disillusionment. All of these can rob us of our commitment to our cause of recovery. Courage gives a place for our commitment to save us.

There will be Gethsemane moments, when you struggle to bear the burden of your healing. When we face these moments with the mental and moral strength of courage, commitment, and faith, they strengthen us, even sanctify us, and become profound healing moments. When we can persevere and withstand, danger, fear, or difficulty that we encounter on our journey of recovery, it signals to the Savior that we are ready for his healing touch.

Senator John McCain asks: *What is indispensable to courage?*

Virtuousness, an active conscience, a love of dignity, a sense of duty that provokes the experience of shame when it is disobeyed, a perspective that ranks the objects of courage higher than its penalties, a capacity for outrage, a seeking nature, hope and the desire and willingness to have courage.

An addict would be lucky to find even one of these qualities in his character. These are skills, beliefs and attitudes that we often must nurture and grow within us. McCain warns: *Courage is not always certain.* We are not always sure why courage surfaces, in fact McCain continues: *There is only one thing that we can claim with complete confidence is indispensable to courage, that must be present for courage to exist: fear. You must be afraid to have courage* (McCain, 2004).

Not to worry. Addicts have fear. Fear of their feelings, of what others think, fear of their demons, fear of losing their comforter, fear of failing, fear of losing themselves, and even fear of finding themselves. We will not ever be lacking in opportunities to display courage, because our fear is never very far away.

Remember the Savior, He is one reason that we can have courage; our faith in Him grows courage. Think of His encouraging words that help us take courage: *In the world ye shall have tribulation: but be of good cheer; I have overcome the world* (John 16: 33).

It is a given that we will face struggles in our lives, that life will be difficult, that we will, at times, feel fear, but the good news is that we can survive it all. He has overcome the world and, if we follow Him, we also shall overcome the tribulation we face. He set a tremendous example for us: *I remember being with President Harold B. Lee in the Garden of Gethsemane in Jerusalem. We could sense, if only in a very small degree, the terrible struggle that took place there, a struggle so intense, as Jesus wrestled alone in the spirit, that blood came from every pore* (see Luke 22:44, D & C 19:18). *We recalled the betrayal by one who had been called to a position of trust. We recalled that evil men laid brutal hands upon the Son of God. We recalled that lonely figure on the cross, crying out in anguish, "My God, my God, why hast thou forsaken me?"* (Matt. 27:46). *Yet, courageously, the Savior of the world moved forward to bring about the Atonement in our behalf* (Hinckley, 2001).

Accountability. Recovery is impossible without accountability and its required honesty. We can maintain the appearance of recovery, make it look like all is well and that we are changing, but it is all smoke and mirrors without the rigorous honesty of accountability. You will need to be more accountable than you have ever been in your life, ridiculously accountable.

Accountability comes into play because we have free agency.

Of course, one's agency is of little productive value unless it is accompanied by knowledge and understanding. When knowledge and understanding are combined with agency, a condition is achieved that we call accountability (Larsen, 1981).

Addiction is an attempt to live life outside of accountability. It is the act of avoiding responsibility and the laws of righteousness, and when we ignore the knowledge and understanding we have gained, we are living in denial. Satan thought that was a great plan. He wanted a world without accountability, where no one had to shoulder responsibility for their actions. Such a world would be the perfect petri dish for growing pride. Honest, complete accountability is the number one defense we have against the devastating effects of pride, because holding ourselves accountable requires healthy doses of humility.

Elaine Cannon said that: *Accountability is the natural product of agency and is the basis of the plan of life. We are responsible for our own actions and accountable to God for what we choose to do with our lives. Life is God's gift to us, and what we do with it is our gift to him.*

In Galatians we read, "Be not deceived; God is not mocked: for whatsoever a man soweth, that shall he also reap." (Gal. 6:7) ... translated into simple idiom that means that if you pick up one end of a stick, you pick up the other. When you pick a path, you choose the place it leads to (Cannon, 1983).

When we choose the path that leads to God and hold ourselves accountable to Him, we are announcing that we believe in Him and His existence. This means we are willing to subject ourselves to Him. When we confess to Him, we are overcoming the pride that would keep us from Him, which in turn, keeps us from recovery and healing.

Elder Dennis Neuenschwander suggested our confessions *facilitate our learning about Him and ultimately bring us to Him.* When we are accountable, we assume responsibility for our own actions. Elder Neuenschwander explains what happens when we assume responsibility for our actions:

It is one of the strongest indicators that we are becoming more like Him. We cannot develop ourselves spiritually by blaming another for our condition. There comes a time in our lives temporally and spiritually, when we must assume responsibility for our choices (Neuenschwander, 1999).

When we can exorcise the lies out of our heart by being accountable to ourselves and God, we free ourselves of their burden. The weight of our misdeeds, secrets and shortcomings can be staggering. As we continually hold ourselves to the high standards of recovery, we are placing recovery above our addiction. We are saying once again, my choice is recovery over using. That choice made consistently and continually will bring us to healing.

Accountability keeps us safe from our addiction's love of isolation, justification, rationalization, denial and our own love affair with pride. Accountability will keep us from being derailed.

These four Attitudes of Recovery are powerful implements and weapons for our war on our addiction. They can make us equal and fit for the battle. They give us power and maximize our abilities. Without them, we are naked and defenseless. Without them, we have no chance.

Packing the Boat

Now that we have learned of the existence of the Waters of Recovery, it is time to enter them. We aren't leaving quite yet, because there are a few things we need to do to prepare for our journey. One of the first things we need to do to prepare is to define two key points or lines on the river.

One is the point at which the waterfall occurs for you. It is your bottom line. It defines when you have acted out. It is the line that, if crossed, means we have lost our sobriety. For the alcoholic it is taking a drink or, for the heroin addict, it is shooting up. It is important to establish this point before you move on so you can actively maintain your bottom line (meaning you have not acted out or otherwise crossed your bottom line.) It is the defining point of your sobriety, and when you violate it, sobriety is lost.

The other key demarcation is the line that defines the beginning of the safe Waters of Recovery. Above that line we are out of our addiction and free from the pull of the falls. When we cross that line and move downstream, we have entered into our addictive behaviors. This means we are in our addiction, and we begin feeling the pull of the falls and become susceptible to its power. This puts our sobriety at risk. Our addiction gains strength as we move downstream in these waters. It is critical to develop an awareness of where that safe line is and to monitor where we are in relation to it.

The territory between our safe line and our bottom line is full of thoughts, behaviors, emotions, involvements and activities that encourage or facilitate our addiction. We know these well; they are old friends, and they are the rituals that we follow to act out. They are what we have to avoid or change in order to heal. These are the waters we must learn to steer clear of, because, while acting out is accomplished at the falls, the process begins when we cross our safe line in the river.

It is now time to say goodbye to your addiction. We are set to embark on the miraculous journey of healing, self discovery, recovery and coming to Christ. There are some things you won't be needing on this journey, your drug of choice, for example. This is where we leave it.

When we end any relationship, it is appropriate to have some closure and say goodbye. After all, you and your drug of choice have been through a lot together. You have had some relationship. You are quite the old friends. At times you have been inseparable. You really should explain to this friend why you won't be around anymore.

Johnny was a long time porn addict. This is the Goodbye Letter he wrote to his addiction:

> *Well, Sleaze...it is time for us to part. It all started out so well. You were just a lot of fun. Exhilarating, really. I don't even know when you turned your back on me and started taking instead of giving. I got so I couldn't get through a day without you, and that wasn't what I signed on for.*
>
> *I thought I would be able to just walk away someday, that I would grow out of you. I really underestimated you*

and misjudged your intentions. You wanted all of me. You left no room for anything else. I didn't realize what you were doing; I thought we were just having fun, a few laughs, blowing off some steam and stress. And I let you get away with it. I just turned a blind eye to what you were doing to me.

And then there was my job. They weren't too happy I was seeing you on their time. I really needed that job. I worked hard for it. And it was gone in a New York minute when they caught me with you. My wife left too. The relationship you and I had destroyed her. She took the kids when I couldn't leave you alone.

What made me think you were worth that?

Man, I tried to walk away, but you really had your hooks in me. You know what really stinks? You aren't even real. All you've got going for you is lust and I realize now that isn't enough. Man, I hate you. I hate that you betrayed me, No, I hate that I betrayed myself and the ones I love. I have been such a fool.

But, no more. This is goodbye, sleaze. I won't be back!

Later in this chapter, in the Rules of Early Recovery section, you will learn that you should maintain a Recovery Journal. One of the first entries in your Recovery Journal should be your Goodbye Letter to your drug of choice. In this letter, talk about why you are saying goodbye, what you want to accomplish in recovery, what you have lost, the price you have paid for addiction, and any other thoughts and feelings you might have.

As with any journey, saying goodbye is the beginning point of the journey to recovery. On this journey, we have rules. Think of them as instructions for your success. Addicts who embark on this upstream journey will be in new territory. These will be new, unknown waters. They are not, however, uncharted. Others have successfully made the journey and have left us with directions of what to do, as well as warnings of what to avoid. They are the Rules of Recovery.

The Rules of Early Recovery

1. Shut up and do the work. Your best thinking got you here, so don't try to think your way out. Just get humble—very, very humble—and teachable and do the work of recovery.

2. Don't believe you own BS. Denial has many voices.

3. Make confession, full and complete. When you kill the secrets, you begin to kill the addiction.

4. Remove all access to your addiction. Destroy any sources, contacts or relationships that were part of your acting out. Throw out the trash!

5. Start working the Twelve Steps.

6. Turn your will and your life over to the Savior for His care and keeping (and leave it there!) Submit, submit, submit. Develop an attitude of submission (Step three of the Twelve Steps).

7. Find support groups, a sponsor and therapists who understand addiction and your faith. Your recovery is like a jigsaw puzzle, you will find pieces (answers) in many places.

8. Establish and maintain sobriety.

9. Keep a Recovery Journal.

10. Find your feelings. Reconnect with your emotional self.

11. Move from your emotionally based decision-making process to a spiritually based decision-making process.

12. Become ridiculously accountable.

13. Begin a quest to find serenity, a benchmark of recovery.

1. **Shut up and do the work. Your best thinking got you here, so don't try to think your way out. Just get humble, very very humble and teachable and do the work of recovery.**

Shut up and do the work. That may sound a bit harsh to some. There is a very important point in it. We know how to be addicts. We are very good at it. We are not very good at recovery. In fact, part of us doesn't like the idea of recovery at all. Our addict within is going to fight this process, sometimes every step of the way. We need to take away our addict's power and control over us. Because you are the author of the rationalizations and justifications that empower your addict, it is very difficult for you to change the direction of your behaviors. You speak the language that has created your addiction. You need to learn to speak the language of recovery. You need to learn that from others. Adopt a submissive, teachable attitude. It opens the gates to the Waters of Recovery.

The Spirit will be a tremendous source of teaching. You will feel epiphanies or "Aha" moments, moments of learning, growth, clarity and understanding. A submissive, teachable attitude will keep those channels of spiritual communication open for you.

As for YOUR best thinking: It did take you to the precipice of the waterfalls and beyond. Denial and thinking errors have devastated your decision-making process. It is time to seek the advice and counsel of others who have successfully traveled this same road.

Addicts don't heal alone AA states, and this is a flat-out promise.

Find out what others have done to win the battle with their addiction and then follow their path. *The way of a fool is right in his own eyes: but he that hearkeneth unto counsel is wise* (Proverbs 12:15). Being *right in his own eyes* is a trap that binds the addict to his addiction. We must learn to look through the eyes of others, to see what they see, and then *hearken unto their counsel* to find our way out of our addiction.

In those early days of accepting that we are, indeed, an addict, and then confronting our situation, we often underestimate the power of our adversary. One of AA's gems states that *half measures avail us nothing!* As one addict put it: *Three quarter measures aren't much good either.* Overcoming addiction is often the fight of our lives. It will require all of our strength, faith, courage and wisdom. We will also need the Recovery Attitudes of Willingness, Commitment, Courage, and Accountability, and we must be fanatical in maintaining them. Addiction has been labeled a *cunning and baffling* disease (Bill W., 2001). Underestimating what is required to recover is a very common problem for those in the Discovery Phase of the process.

A Parable of Recovery

An old farm boy lived at the base of a sizable hill. In the old days it had been logged, and there was a very steep and rough road to the top left over from those days. It looked more like a trail really, not well defined, sloughed in by time. But it looked inviting to the farm boy in his four-wheel drive pickup. He always enjoyed a good, challenging ride and, after walking the trail, he decided it might be possible for a very good driver in a very good pickup to make it to the top.

Well, he knew he was a good driver, as good as any around, and he loved and trusted his old truck, she'd be up to the task like no other truck he knew! So, he made his decision; he would try to drive to the top of the hill.

He got dressed in his four-wheelin' garb, boots and rain pants for sloggin' through whatever he might come across, his driving gloves and googles. He gathered his come-along and fired up old Betsey. She certainly sounded up to the challenge, purrin' like a 400-horsepower kitten wanting to turn into a mountain lion.

Because he was a bit cautious, his first attempt only got him about a quarter of the way up the hill. He didn't know the road very well, so didn't know where to slow down, where to gun it. But his failure only made him more resolved to get to the top. So he backed down and started over.

This time he gave Betsey a lot more gas and a lot less brake but still only got one halfway up the hill. "Hmmmm, this is tougher than I thought" he muttered as he backed down the hill. He thought about what else he could do. He disconnected the exhaust to get a bit more horsepower, put on tire chains for better traction, and vowed to go all out with the gas. Still in spite of all his additional efforts, he could only get three quarters of the way up the hill.

He was very frustrated, and, as he backed down the hill, he thought, "Toughest dang hill I ever saw!" His resolve only increased in the face of his failures. He was going to drive to the top of this hill, no matter what it took. As he reached the bottom of the hill, he backed right on past his old starting place. Way past. "If I can build up enough momentum ...," he surmised, and he gave himself and extra 100 yards or so to really build up some speed.

So he took off, "hell-bent for election," as Pa used to say. He hit the bottom of the hill with tremendous speed, flew over holes and ruts, barely clung to the hill as he rounded the corners, but he passed his old "best" and made it to the top of the hill. With a great deal of satisfaction he contemplated his victory. "I just didn't get a big enough run at it."

The story of recovery and relapse is a lot like that of our old country farm boy. We know we are in for a struggle, but we naively think we are fit for the battle. When we slip or fail we might renew our efforts with a bit more determination, perhaps wiser about the strength of our adversary. We try again, adding horsepower and tools to help us. Over and over, we may find ourselves at the bottom of the hill to begin the quest once more.

With each new attempt we gain renewed conviction and motivation, added tools and knowledge of what we are up against. When we use every tool, every ability, every bit of strength, and when we get a good enough run at it, we may make it to the top.

Follow Rule Number One. Quiet your addict, humble yourself, become teachable and roll up your sleeves and undertake the work of recovery.

2. Don't believe you own BS. Denial has many voices.

To allow themselves to experience the comfort of acting out in their lives, addicts employ the truth-twisting and reality-bending benefits of denial. Denial is the hall pass to our addiction. Denial can help us justify our acting out or even hide it completely, even from our own eyes. Remember Ron? "I was NOT a sex addict. I was NOT that guy!" He really didn't believe he was an addict, until he recognized that he was doing what a sex addict does. Some of the hardest work of recovery is in recognizing, coming to terms with, and gaining freedom from the addict's patterns of denial.

Unfortunately, we lie to ourselves as much as we lie to others. "I need this," or "No one will know," or even, "I am not hurting anyone." The list of thinking errors or denial patterns is very long. Addicts are very creative people. Often, the more intelligent they are, the better addicts they become. Terence Gorski, MA, has identified the patterns of denial in his book, *Denial Management Counseling* (Gorski 2000). He states these patterns as:

Minimizing and Absolute Denial

Denial by Avoidance

Denial by Rationalization

Denial by Blaming

Denial by Comparing

I am Better; Therefore, I am Well, Denial

Denial by Hopelessness

Denial by Right

Minimizing and Absolute Denial. Some addicts—like our friend, Ron, in the example shared previously—use Absolute Denial, *I am NOT that guy!* He also throws in a little Minimizing for good measure, *Yes, I had some problems with affairs, but ..*

One of the classic reasons that individuals cannot recognize themselves as addicts is that they don't meet their definition or their mind's picture of what an addict is. It is the perfect setup for Minimizing:

Elton was a pretty high-functioning alcoholic. He taught high school, didn't miss work, and was very well respected by both colleagues and students. In Elton's mind an alcoholic was the guy in that Christmas movie with

Jimmy Stewart. You know the one—the unshaven guy, disheveled, stumbling in and out of bars, begging for drinks. Elton was nothing like that, so there was no way he could convict himself of being a drunk. The reality is, alcoholics come in all kinds of packages. Elton came to understand this when he was driving home from work with a very high blood/alcohol content and was the cause of a terrible accident that took someone's life. He couldn't deny that he was a drunk any longer.

An extreme example of Absolute Denial is given by an undercover agent on the Drug Task Force in Clark County, Washington:

If we are following a car with marijuana, cocaine or heroin, as soon as we are discovered, windows come down and drugs fly out the window; however, meth users believe they won't get caught.

When I pull over a meth guy, and I get him out of the car, I ask, "Do you have any drugs on you?" Invariably the answer is no. When I search his pants, and a stash is found, he instantly blurts out, "These aren't my pants!"

Now, my first question upon stopping a suspect is, "Uhh, are those your pants?"

Meth addicts can really bend reality with denial. Their drug of choice profoundly harms the brain, creating a surge of thinking errors. The thinking and denial patterns progress to a point of being so distorted and illogical that anyone else can easily recognize the lie. The meth addict thinks it is more than believable. He is quite indignant when we can't accept his explanation. This is Absolute Denial on steroids! The meth addict is so trapped in his thinking that getting out is impossible without a great deal of help, but, too often, he doesn't see that help as necessary.

It is not uncommon to hear a heavy drug user minimize by saying:

No way I am an addict. I don't use needles. This kind of thinking keeps the addict in the "what I am doing is not that bad" category! It allows him to escape the reality of who he has become.

Shary and Frank had been married almost 15 year. They had one child and the appearance of the picture-perfect relationship. *Everyone loved my husband,* Shary thought. Then she found a long history of e-mails and Internet activity that painted a picture of many affairs and betrayals. When she did so, Frank responded with a very common form of absolute denial, which looks like this:

> *When I confronted him, it was terrible. He accused me of spying on him and of violating his privacy.*
> *"You owe me an explanation," I said.*
> *He was angry and hostile and said he didn't owe me anything. He thought that he hadn't done anything wrong.*
> *You would think he caught me doing all those things by the way he was acting! He tried to kick us out of the house and has been taking everything that he can. He is being vicious. The one person that I thought I could always count on and trust was leading a secret life.*

Addicts love to use anger and indignation as an alternative to admitting their addictions. As in Shary's case, it can get ugly. Many spouses and friends—in their confusion, hurt and fear—back down from the angry, bellowing addict. Being loud and angry doesn't change anything. If you are an addict, you are an addict, no matter how loud you beller.

Denial by Avoidance. Avoidance is happy to talk about anything that does not involve drug or alcohol use. An avoider has become an expert at manipulation to keep the spotlight off of him and his use. He uses a variety of techniques to practice his form of denial.

He is great at changing the focus by asking provocative questions that put attention on others. He loves to put others down, because this gets him a double payoff. It makes him feel better about himself, and it focuses attention away from his use. He might say: *So, I saw the cops over* at your house last week...what was going on? Or, John said you weren't at the AA meeting last night and he thought you were out drinking instead ... so what's going on?

Users of Avoidance become masters at being vague. *I guess, maybe, I drink socially, I smoke occasionally,* is the flavor of their conversation. They are purposefully unspecific and unclear to avoid others knowing their reality (Najavits, 2002).

Avoiders may also like to create a lot of drama. They love to keep things stirred up, always at the expense of others. The benefit, again, is that this creates a smokescreen that helps hide their own behaviors and situation from public knowledge.

Denial by Rationalization. The addict who uses Rationalization is one who claims to always have a good reason for what he does.

Excuses were created for rationalizers: *I drink because I am depressed. Pot is the only thing that relieves the pain.* Rationalizers punch their own ticket to get on the addiction train. They rationalize themselves right into trouble.

Good rationalizers have enough truth and logic that we accept what they say without question. Individuals of high intellect are especially good at this form of denial.

Denial by Blaming. Blamers have never been at fault for anything. There is always someone or something else to blame. Blamers create resentment to their advantage. *Your nagging is impossible to live with ... who wouldn't drink?* By creating a victim role for themselves, they feel justified in using. Everyone wants to feel sympathy for a victim. We want to be nice people. Blamers set us up, making us feel just enough sympathy for them that we do not question their solutions.

Denial by Comparing. Those that use Comparing are close cousins to the minimizers. They take comfort in the fact that they aren't as bad as *that guy.* They often take the next step in logic and deduce for themselves that they are not addicts.

John's brother was in and out of rehab most of his adult life. He seemed unable to shake the demons. John spent a great deal of time and money trying to help his brother. It never occurred to him that he was also an alcoholic (even while drinking a fifth a day), because he didn't have the problems his brother did.

Comparing sounds like this: *Yeah, I use some, but I'm not out of control, I am sure not like that tweaked out Jerry. Now that guy has a problem, you should be talking to him!* The addict is very comforted that he is not Jerry, even to the point that he can completely excuse his own addiction as not that bad. This isn't very far from: *I do not have a problem.*

I am Better, Therefore, I am Well, Denial. There is a phenomenon in recovery that creates the "I am Better, Therefore, I am Well" denial pattern. When a person begins recovery with some sincerity, initial progress is made. There are immediate results. Clarity begins to return, guilt and shame are eased, and the addict feels better than they have felt for some time. After this, it is easy for the belief to come that healing has happened and is accomplished. They are sure that their using wasn't that bad, and they often believe they can use on a limited basis without harm. Those who fall into this trap, are soon back in their addictive behaviors.

Denial by Hopelessness. Hopelessness is especially problematic for long-time addicts. A person can only try to quit so many times without success before they reach a point where they believe that quitting is not possible. Giving up hope soon follows. When hope is lost, the addiction game has moved to a whole new level, and recovery becomes much more difficult. Even reaching out or seeking help becomes impractical in the addict's mind.

Addicts affected by hopelessness can allow themselves unlimited involvement in their addiction. After all, there is nothing that can be done. They believe: *This is my fate.*

Denial by Right. This addict recognizes what he is doing, admits his addiction, but claims the right to continue his self destruction. *I have the right to kill myself! Leave me alone!* Denial by Right is a very common pattern among adolescent males and is often founded on anger and shame.

Throughout the process of recovery when we encounter denial, we should apply the Recovery Attitude of Accountability. Accountability is the antidote for denial.

We should measure recovery progress in terms of behavior and not words. Addicts are master word manipulators. Words can easily paint any picture we wish. That is why denial serves the addict's purpose. Behaviors reveal the true intention of the heart. Whether with ourselves or those with whom we are trying to rebuild relationships, don't listen to the words. Watch the behaviors.

It is easy for an addict to say: *I am no longer going to lie to you.* However, the most often uttered words of spouses who have believed that and then been disappointed, yet again, are something like: *But he said he had changed.* The words of an addict cannot be trusted. Only consistent, reliable behavior can be believed. The truth and the reality will be revealed over time, as honesty is displayed repeatedly and dishonesty is absent.

Denial patterns are presented when the client uses his addict voice. *I am not as bad as John. I don't have a problem. I am past help.* A very important therapeutic moment occurs when a client reveals his addict's voice. In those moments, the clinician has the opportunity to further recovery by pointing out these statements and identifying them for what they are. This may serve to introduce the client to his addict within, a meeting that is often quite surprising to the addict.

3. **Make confession, full and complete. When you kill the secrets you begin to kill the addiction.**

The headwaters of addiction are found in isolation. We begin to leave our addiction when we can destroy the isolation and get out of our secret world, where the art of self destruction is being practiced by our secret self. Our addiction withers when the light of truth beams upon it. That light is turned on by confession. It is turned off by secrecy.

So we strike the first blows against our addiction with confession. Confession begins to establish Accountability. As established previously in this book, one of the two goals of the Recovery Phase is to bring ourselves to Christ. A true, honest and willing confession is the first step in opening that door. *Why is confession essential? First, because the Lord commanded it, and secondly, because the offender cannot live and participate in the Kingdom of God, to receive the blessings therefrom with a lie in his heart* (Richards, 1954).

Look at those *who will not or do not, confess their transgressions. Their lives are filled with bitterness, anger, impatience, and harsh judgment toward others and with fierce justification of their actions. In the absence of true and full confession, we witness the presence of pride and a lack of responsibility for their own actions* (Neuenschwander, 1999).

The *Whitebook* of Sexaholics Anonymous illustrates the importance and value of confession by saying: *The spiritual connection begins here. By first disconnecting from what we did. And we disconnect from it by sending it away from us as we tell it. This is the point of breakthrough.*

A point of breakthrough! We are making our first progress out of our addiction. *The spiritual connection begins here.* If we are seeking the Savior and His healing powers, this is where we start to access Him. Accomplishing a full and true confession moves us upstream away from the falls of acting out. As we move upstream, by killing the secrets with confession, we have begun to kill the addiction.

Some elements of confession can be tricky business. We can confess to the wrong people, hurting them, and we can confess for the wrong reasons, hurting ourselves. We should carefully confess the appropriate things to the appropriate people.

Our confession to the bishop of our ward should include the acts committed, the period of time involved, frequency and any innocents that our behaviors harmed. Graphic details serve no purpose and are not necessary. The bishop will guide you through the experience and ask any relevant questions that are needed to give him the information that he needs to fulfill his office as judge in Israel. Just go with a humble, open heart.

When we confess to a spouse, we again need to be forthright and open. Graphic details, or even details that include places and times, are most often counterproductive. A spouse whose husband had engaged in repeated affairs said of his confession:

I found I was better off not knowing many details. Details just sucked me into a police women role, and a neverending list of questions, the answers of which really didn't matter. Landmarks that he mentioned to me became places that I avoided. Many of the details caused me more pain than consolation.

Some details are helpful and bring healing. Each spouse's comfort level and their need to know may vary significantly. Let the spouse determine how much is enough.

Sometimes we confess for our own self-comfort, even at the expense of others. This seems particularly true for sex addicts, who have held their many secrets for a long time. Confession is very comforting to them. They have finally off-loaded a tremendous burden. It is euphoric. The soul is soothed by the act of confession. Some can't stop confessing! They want to confess to everyone! They find themselves confessing over and over to whoever will listen. They are trying to recreate that comfort for their souls.

However, confessions are not necessarily soothing to the people who hear them. Instead, they can be burdens. Those in authority, ordained to hear confessions, are prepared and trained in what to do with them. Our friends and family members are not. If we are asking them to process difficult and burdensome material so that we can feel better about ourselves, it is a very selfish act. When we are addicts, we are very good at being selfish. Confession is a place where we need to stop being selfish. It is a place to confess the appropriate things to the appropriate people.

Then, there is Fred's story:

Fred came forward and confessed that he had had an affair but left out a similar transgression that had happened years earlier with another member of his local congregation. He rationalized that he was protecting her. Fred faced Church disciplinary action and, over time, regained his Church standing. A year or so later, his earlier affair became known and Fred faced another council with conse-quences and embarrassment that he could have avoided by making a full and complete original confession.

Some are tempted to fudge on their confessions. When we hold back, or hold on to part of our secrets, we might as well hold onto all of them. The only way we can access the Waters of Recovery that surround the Savior is through honest and complete confession. Otherwise, we are not completely committed to healing. Remember, *half measures avail us nothing.* Our own self-judgment will undermine our recovery and sobriety. The Lord cannot make his healing touch available to us if we are not complete in our submission and humility.

4. **Remove all access to your addiction. Destroy any sources, contacts or relationships that were part of your acting out. Throw out the trash!**

According to this Rule of Recovery, in order to remain in the eddies and far away from the waterfalls, we also need to eliminate our access to our drug of choice.

Will wanted to go on a mission. He was a great kid. He was bright and had a strong testimony. He was a hard worker and had already saved enough money to pay for his mission. He was past 19 years of age and starting to grow very tired of the question, "When are you leaving?" Will struggled with pornography. His Stake President was trying to work with him and set a sobriety goal that would allow his papers to be sent in. His addiction counselor suggested that the family install a history program on the computer that Will could not tamper with. His family was resistant, feeling that Will should be able to control himself. The counselor was also aware that Will had viewed porn with his phone and suggested that he change his service

> plan so that he did not have Internet access. Will was slow to make the change, thinking it wasn't going to be a problem again, and made the excuse that he used the Internet on his phone for other things and needed it. (*This is how denial works.*)
>
> Will was nearing his sobriety goal when he slipped by accessing his favorite porn site with his phone. Following that, his sobriety was lost several other times when he accessed porn on the family computer. ("*They will never know,*" he rationalized.) Removing his access and eliminating the chance of secrecy would have been a very simple solution. In fact, it was the solution. It just took six months for him to accept the necessity of it.

Getting rid of all access means ALL access. Old relationships can be especially dangerous to our sobriety.

> John was a true junkie. A heroin addict. Though he was only 26, he had gotten a very early start through his mother's addiction. John had finally broken away and was in his second month of sobriety. This was something he had only been able to achieve previously when he was locked up in jail. John was working and had just cashed his first paycheck and was walking home. He was not thinking about using.
>
> John explains: *I mean I was feeling as sober as I could feel. I liked having a little money in my pocket. I had no intention of using. I was minding my own business. And up pulls a carload of my user friends going to get high. When they said, "Do you want to go?" I was in the car and not thinking about being sober anymore.*

John added the following insight: *If I put myself in certain situations and settings, I am going to use.*

One aspect of recovery is learning not to put ourselves in those situations and settings. All addicts have a ritualistic piece to their acting out. The progression of the ritual, gives our acting out a predictability. Understanding the predictability of our addiction can help us build sobriety and prevent relapse. When does our addict appear? Under what circumstances does our addict take control? Recognizing those situations and moments gives us a blueprint for part of our recovery. These are items to mark for demolition or elimination, so that the construction of recovery can begin.

We have to separate ourselves from user friends and our using environment. Sometimes, just driving by the old favorite tavern is enough to pull the alcoholic's car in the parking lot. One client, who acted in bookstores, would be drawn into the store if the parking lot was full of cars. He was curious about who was there to act out with. An empty parking lot did not tempt him. A full lot meant certain acting out. His best solution, of course, was to take a different route and not see the parking lot full or empty.

Knowing when we won't act out can be just as helpful as knowing when we will. When are the times and situations where my addict does not appear? These are the safe times. These are the moments that build sobriety. When we recognize them, we can begin to fill our lives with safety, build sobriety and begin to escape our addiction.

So throw out the trash! Get rid of your porn stash, flush your remaining drugs, throw out your dealer's phone number and destroy any contact information for acting out friends. Whatever the addiction, get rid of the drug of choice and all of its connections in your life yes, ALL.

Start Working the Twelve Steps.

Step work, working the Twelve Steps, is at the core of the Church's *Addiction Recovery Program*. Attending Twelve Step meetings, obtaining a sponsor, prayerfully reading and studying the workbook, and working through the Twelve Steps are key elements of building on sobriety and obtaining recovery. The steps focus on our spiritual awakening, bringing us to Christ and helping us live our lives in a way that will keep us within His influence. In keeping with that goal, the Twelve Steps are a work that is never really completed.

Originally published in *The Big Book* by a fledgling society called Alcoholics Anonymous in 1939, the Twelve Steps have been accepted and followed by hundreds of self-help organizations since then. Literally millions of people have benefited from following them. The steps have stood the test of time.

Those who work the steps are guided to a spiritual awakening. The Twelve Steps have an Articles-of-Faith-type of quality. They outline the path of recovery and describe how we may accomplish it. These steps do not conflict with the gospel and their adherence actually will stimulate the practice of your religion.

> *The Big Book states: The great fact is just this, and nothing else. That we [in the AA fellowship] have had deep and effective spiritual experiences which have revolutionized our whole attitude toward life, toward our fellows, and toward God's universe. The central fact of our lives today is the absolute certainty that our Creator entered into our hearts and lives in a way which is indeed miraculous. He has commenced to accomplish those things for us which we could never do by ourselves. (Bill W. 2001)*

The back story of the *Big Book* and the founding of AA involves two hopeless alcoholics, who—after many years of failed attempts at sobriety—met, and found recovery, by turning to God and serving others. In his own struggle, years before he met Dr. Bob, Bill W. decided he would bring drunks off the streets of New York into his home and feed and clothe them while helping them recover. He worked tirelessly for six months, many passed through his home and all returned to drunkenness. Dejected he went to his wife to report his failure.

Dear, none of them are sober, he said.

No Bill, but you are! she responded in her wisdom.

The understanding that serving others can help us recover and find healing was born. The story of how the Twelve Steps came about is both fascinating and miraculous, and the Lord's influence is found throughout that history.

Scott Peck MD, said of understanding of the value of the Twelve Step movement: *Thus I believe the greatest positive event of the twentieth century occurred in Akron, Ohio, on June 10, 1935, when Bill W. and Dr. Bob convened the first AA meeting. It was not only the beginning of the self-help movement and the beginning of the integration of science and spirituality at a grass-roots level, but also the beginning of the integration of the community movement. That is the reason why I think of addiction as the sacred disease. When my AA friends and I get together, we often come to conclude that, very probably, God deliberately created the disorder of alcoholism in order to create alcoholics, in order that these alcoholics might create AA, and thereby spearhead the community movement which is going to be the salvation not only of alcoholics and addicts but of us all.*

Bill W. came to understand the plight of alcoholism and addiction on a very personal basis. In his life struggle, he also came to understand the solution.

Lack of power, that was our dilemma. We had to find a power by which we could live and heal, and it had to be a Power greater than ourselves.

But where and how were we to find this Power? Well that is exactly what [The Big Book] *is all about. Its main object is to enable you to find a Power greater than yourself which will solve your problem* (Scott Peck 1993).

Letting the Savior solve our problem is how we heal. Figuring out the how of that, and making the changes in our lives that let Him do that, is the work of recovery. Turning our mind and will over to Him for His care and keeping puts us squarely on the path. If we can let our will be swallowed up by His will, we find the strength we need to do the work of recovery. Finding strength by submission may seem like strange doctrine. Such is the result of giving up our need to control. It opens the floodgates, allowing recovery to flow to us.

The Twelve Steps
(As found in the LDS Recovery Program Workbook)

Step 1. Admit that you, of yourself, are powerless to overcome your addictions and that your life has become unmanageable.

Step 2. Come to believe that the power of God can restore you to complete spiritual health.

Step 3. Decide to turn your will and your life over to the care of God the Eternal Father and His Son, Jesus Christ.

Step 4. Make a searching and fearless written moral inventory of yourself.

Step 5. Admit to yourself, to you Heavenly Father in the name of Jesus Christ, to proper priesthood authority and to another person the exact nature of your wrongs.

Step 6. Become entirely ready to have God remove all your character weakness.

Step 7. Humbly ask Heavenly Father to remove your shortcomings.

Step 8. Make a written list of all persons you have harmed and become willing to make restitution to them.

Step 9. Wherever possible, make direct restitution to all persons you have harmed.

Step 10. Continue to take personal inventory, and when you are wrong promptly admit it.

Step 11. Seek through prayer and meditation to know the Lord's will and to have the power to carry it out.

Step 12. Having had a spiritual awakening as a result of the Atonement of Jesus Christ, share this message with others and practice these principles in all you do (LDS Family, Addiction Recovery Program).

The ultimate quest of the Twelve Steps is to help us have a spiritual awakening, an awakening that puts us in conscious contact with our God and delivers us from our addictive behaviors. It is not the purpose of this writer to provide a *how-to* manual for working the steps (that information is available elsewhere), but it is important that we understand some of the benefits derived from working the steps.

Steps 1 through 3 can be cryptically described as: *I can't solve this problem, but the Savior can, and I will let Him.* Embracing that idea and learning what that implies (how that translates) in our daily walk is the work of the first three steps.

There is tremendous value in Steps 4 and 5, which involve making our searching and fearless moral inventory and sharing it with selected others. These steps attack our shame and help us heal. Shame is something many struggle to give up. One of the most common deflectors encountered clinically, is the statement in the client's mind: *Yes, but if you really knew me. What you're saying is sort of true, but if you really understood who I am or what I have done ...* The client uses this statement, without realizing that it compromises his healing progress and therapeutic direction.

These kinds of statements keep us in our shame, which, in turn, keeps us in our addiction. When we use such statements, we are discounting the Savior's love for us and the ability of those who love us to forgive. We are discounting ourselves. That moves us away from Him.

When we completely reveal ourselves and our inventory, we kill all of our secrets. When we find, in spite of the secrets, that we are still loved and accepted, our shame (the belief that there is something wrong with us) begins to wither and die. It can only thrive in our secret, dark thoughts and beliefs.

What is shame? It is more than a feeling. It is a set of physical responses (such as looking down or blushing) combined with predictable actions (such as hiding or withdrawing from others), uncomfortable thoughts (such as I am a failure in life), spiritual despair. Our definition of shame is that it is a painful belief in one's basic defectiveness as a human being (Potter-Efron, 1989).

Shame, or this *spiritual despair,* is a toxic inhibitor to recovery to say nothing of how it obstructs our relationship with the Savior. We begin to eliminate shame and free ourselves to move to Him when we find the acceptance of others by completing these steps. We then have the chance to accept ourselves.

A word of caution about confession and self disclosure: When it comes to revealing our personal inventory, there are valid reasons for being very cautious about this self-disclosure, making sure that we confess in the proper way and to the appropriate people. Maintaining confidentiality should be of paramount concern, so that the innocents in our lives are not hurt. We also should not fall into the trap of using confession to soothe ourselves at the expense of others.

Steps 8 and 9 provide similar healing as these steps focus on the process of being accountable and making restitution or amends for our past behaviors. We are able to clean up some of the flotsam and jetsam that have accumulated in our addictive wake. We most often have no idea of the burdens that our unresolved matters place on ourselves or others.

Unresolved issues bleed off our emotional strength every day, depleting the resources we need to heal and change our lives. Our emotional capital needs to be spent for healing; it cannot be squandered on old matters. Only when we begin to make amends and free ourselves of the burden, only then, do we gain a sense of what a tremendous load we were carrying!

Steps 10 through 12 touch on daily accountability, the benefits of personal revelation and the healing advantages of service to others. These concepts are discussed at length in other sections of this work.

In the LDS Family Services Addiction Recovery Program's *Guide to Addiction Recovery and Healing*, a single word or phrase is associated with each step, as listed below:

Step 1. Honesty

Step 2. Hope

Step 3. Trust in God

Step 4. Truth

Step 5. Confession

Step 6. Change of Heart

Step 7. Humility

Step 8. Seeking Forgiveness

Step 9. Restitution and Reconciliation

Step 10. Daily Accountability

Step 11. Personal Revelation

Step 12. Service

These are the very attitudes, attributes and actions of recovery.

Some addicts who are members of the Church approach working the Twelve Steps with skepticism. They may say something like: *I am a member of the true Church and I shouldn't have to look any further than that for a spiritual awakening. I don't think I need to work the steps because I already believe in God and have faith that He can heal me.*

This is the voice of your addict. Please apply Early Recovery Rule Number One: *Quiet yourself and start working.*

Turn your will and your life over to the Savior for His care and keeping (and leave it there!) Submit, submit, submit. Develop an Attitude of Willingness. (Step 3 of the Twelve Steps)

Submission is the practice that allows us to know God. When we are able to submit ourselves, we begin to qualify for this statement: *I see that your faith is sufficient that I should heal you* (3 Nephi 17: 8). Submission was introduced by the Savior as a point of doctrine in Matthew 18: 1-3: *Verily I say unto you, Except ye be converted, and become as little children, ye shall not enter into the kingdom of heaven.*

Whosoever therefore shall humble himself as this little child, the same is greatest in the kingdom of heaven.

As He established His church in the Americas, the Savior set forth his doctrine, and, as we read in 3 Nephi 11: 32-38, He repeats Himself three times for clarity.

32. And this is my doctrine...I bear record that the Father commandeth all men, everywhere, to repent and believe on me.

33. And whoso believeth in me and is baptized, the same shall be saved; and they are they who shall inherit the kingdom of God.

37. And again I say...ye must repent, and become as a little child, and be baptized in my name, or ye can in nowise receive these things.

38. And again I say...ye must repent, and be baptized in my name, and become as a little child or ye can in nowise inherit the kingdom of God.

In explaining the doctrine the Father has set forth, Christ is very clear that we must *repent, believe on Him and be baptized.* He adds, in verses 37 and 38, that in this process we must *become as a little child*. In other words, to truly practice the doctrine, we must take on childlike qualities. Mosiah tells us that this means becoming:

Submissive, meek, humble, patient, full of love, willing to submit to all things which the Lord seeth fit to inflict upon him, even as a child doth submit to his father (Mosiah 3:19).

These are the qualities He would have us develop as we come to Him. We must become *submissive, meek, humble, patient, full of love,* and *willing to submit* to the will of the Lord, whatever His *will* for us is.

President Henry B. Eyring shared this example from his own life:

Once, for instance, I prayed through the night to know what I was to choose to do in the morning. I knew that no other choice could have had a greater effect on the lives of others and on my own. I knew what choice looked most comfortable to me. I knew what outcome I wanted. But I could not see the future. I could not see which choice would lead to which outcome. So the risk of being wrong seemed too great to me.

I prayed, but for hours there seemed to be no answer. Just before dawn, a feeling came over me. More than at any time since I had been a child, I felt like one. My heart and my mind seemed to grow very quiet. There was a peace in that inner stillness.

Somewhat to my surprise, I found myself praying, "Heavenly Father, it doesn't matter what I want. I don't care anymore what I want. I only want that Thy will be done. That is all that I want. Please tell me what to do."

In that moment I felt as quiet inside as I had ever felt. And the message came, and I was sure who it was from. It was clear what I was to do. I received no promise of the outcome. There was only the assurance that I was a child who had been told what path led to whatever He wanted for me.

I learned from that experience and countless repetitions that the description of the Holy Ghost as a still, small voice is real. It is poetic, but it is not poetry. Only when my heart has been still and quiet, in submission like a little child, has the Spirit been clearly audible to my heart and mind (Eyring, 2006).

This man of God has found that only when he is able to in submission *like a little child,* then and only then, *has the Spirit been clearly audible to my heart and mind.* If this prophet of God finds childlike submission a prerequisite for the clear, audible communication of the Spirit to his heart and mind, it would seem doubtful that we could attain that kind of communication without that same submission.

If we were in a classroom or group session, at this point I would very likely be hearing from the back of the room: *What about my free agency? All of this talk about submission, turning my mind and will over to the Lord, doesn't that mean I am giving up my free agency?*

Elder Neal A. Maxwell said: *We don't have to go very far before we have to decide which way we should pitch our tent, facing towards the temple or toward Sodom and Gomorra* (Maxwell, 2003). Our free agency is in constant use as we follow the will of the Father in our lives. The use of our free agency keeps our submission intact. The exercising of our free agency, over and over throughout our day, keeps us in the attitude of submission.

Struggling clients often pontificate at length upon the God-given right to free agency and the dangers if one blindly submits to any principle or person. Such tirades and exposition could go on for hours. A client in this state is often angry and even self-righteous. None of the childlike qualities mentioned in Mosiah are present. Then, he reports at the next session that he has not maintained his sobriety. The two events are related, the second a result of the first.

If you struggle with submission, or if you experience the feelings of resistance coming up in the therapeutic process—especially those that bring on some form of anger, contention or contempt—pay attention. These are the issues that cause you difficulty. They are the issues that impede your recovery or have allowed your addiction to exist and flourish in the first place. Resolving these issues is key to your recovery. Don't dismiss or ignore these types of reactions.

In our self-reliant society, admitting we have a problem can be embarrassing. It can make us feel uncomfortable and we can feel there is something wrong with us or that we don't measure up. We have already established that healing without help isn't an option, it doesn't work. Just reaching out for help can often be the most difficult step we encounter. It is a place for us to apply our Recovery Attitudes of Courage and Submission.

John was a former Bishop. His family was very well known and respected in the Church. His parents and grandparents held very responsible and highly visible positions. John initially asked to meet with his addiction counselor in the privacy of his home when his family was away. One of his first concerns was that if people found out he had an addiction, it would be a terrible blight on the family name. It became apparent that he needed to attend the Church's Addiction Recovery meetings. He resisted the notion for nearly half a year based on his fear of who might see him attend. As his addiction persisted, his humility grew, and finally he agreed to go. There were many blessings to John and others in the group from his attendance.

The fear of who might know nearly kept him from those blessings and the healing that has followed. One of the goals of the Attitudes of Willingness and Submission is that we are able to let go of pride and the fear of being judged by others. One addict looks at it this way:

You know that someday they are going to be shouting our sins from the roof tops ... well, I don't have much to worry about, everybody already knows ... I am not afraid of that. His humble approach is an attitude of recovery.

When we take the approach that we care more about healing than about who might know our secrets, we have learned to submit and the Lord knows we are ready to receive his healing touch.

Find support groups, a sponsor and therapists who understand addiction and your faith. Your recovery is like a jigsaw puzzle, you will find pieces (answers) in many places.

It can be helpful to consider recovery as a giant jigsaw puzzle, a puzzle for which we are not given all the pieces. We must find them. They will be found in many places, sometimes quite unlikely places. Don't fall into the trap of believing that healing will come easily. It isn't going to happen over night or after meeting with the Bishop a few times, attending some treatment, or by reading the latest recovery book. Your puzzle is much more complex than that, hence, the need for the Recovery Attitude of Commitment.

Attending groups can be very helpful in the recovery process. Groups generally come in two forms, support or self-help groups, such as AA or the Church's Addiction Recovery Groups, or treatment groups that are centered on come sort of therapeutic approach.

The great value in support groups is that they allow us to gain perspective. We are not alone. Others also struggle as we do. We find strength in being with them. We lean on their support, and we find healing for ourselves by serving them. William said it this way after four months of attending weekly meetings of his local Church Addiction Recovery Group:

> I thought all these years that I was the only guy who struggled with this. What attending the group helped me understand was that I wasn't some weird, broken freak. A lot of good, wonderful people struggle as I do and that made me feel a lot better about myself. Feeling the unconditional love of the group has given me great strength. The other thing is the presence of the Spirit. It is always amazingly strong at group. Feeling the Savior's love for all of us, broken and struggling as we are, has strengthened my love for the Savior and my testimony of His reality.

Ron served as a group facilitator for the Addiction Recovery Program for several years. He says:

> In the beginning I had some very strong ideas about how to recover. I felt restrained by the format of the meetings. I couldn't share all the incredible ideas that I had. Then I noticed something. I was sometimes getting in the way of the Spirit with all my personal recovery ideas. When I started getting out of the way and just trying to

create a place for the Spirit to be welcome, amazing things happened all around the group table. Now I try to shut up and just let Him do His work.

Treatment groups can be a very useful tool for accessing therapeutic help in overcoming addiction. They are an economical way to obtain treatment for addiction and underlying issues. Groups usually follow some sort of therapeutic philosophy that examines issues and guides toward healing. They address issues in a direct manner and are not always designed as support vehicles. Treatment groups can lack the "feel good" elements of support groups and can be confrontational. Our addict can be called out and challenged, which forces us to confront our issues in front of the group.

Individual therapy allows for directly dealing with our issues without the noise that can be generated in the group setting. All the focus is on you and what you are dealing with as well as what you are trying to accomplish. For obvious reasons, this is the most effective form of treatment. It is important that the therapist you choose is knowledgeable about addiction and about your faith. You also need to feel a high level of trust and comfort with this individual. Finding the right person is sometimes not easy.

Remember this about all forms of treatment: Success is up to you, not the treatment provider. Therapist William Howatt states: *No matter what any counselor does, in the end clients will always do what they want.* Other studies show that *there is a direct correlation between the level of motivation and client's success in treatment* (Howatt, 1999).

Individual and group therapy can be tremendous sources of information, direction and healing, but you determine if they are successful. You are the one, after all, who puts the puzzle together.

Sponsors have been a fixture of AA from its inception. Bill W. and Dr. Bob knew that healing comes from helping others. Only those with appropriate sobriety and recovery should act as sponsors. They can be a treasure trove of information and insight. They have an in-the-trenches knowledge of addiction, which can be very helpful as we work the steps of recovery. They can help us find accountability; they are often very good at calling us on our BS when we slip into old patterns of denial. The sponsor also benefits from the relationship and finds his own measure of healing through serving others.

Meeting regularly with your Bishop or Stake President can also be a source of answers. These leaders have a spiritual mantle that allows them access to the Spirit on our behalf. Their counsel should be considered and adopted as you seek healing. They have spiritual messages for you that are not available any other place.

Reading both recovery literature and the scriptures, on a daily basis, can be the source of many answers that we seek. Elder Eyring put it this way:

I will make you a promise about reading the Book of Mormon: you will be drawn to it as you understand that the Lord has embedded in it His message to you. Nephi, Mormon, and Moroni knew that, and those who put it together put in messages for you. The Book was written for you. There are simple direct messages that will tell you how to change. That is what the Book is about. It is a testimony of the Lord, Jesus Christ and the Atonement and how it works in our lives. Change comes by the power of the Atonement because of studying this book (Eyring, 2004).

Go find the messages the Lord has placed there for you. They will lie there, unnoticed and undelivered, if you do not open the book and read.

Daily reading of recovery literature reminds us of our task at hand and reminds us of what we can do to facilitate the Lord's healing process in our lives. The literature can help us fill our toolbox with recovery tools, tools that are useful as we move upstream.

Prayer is also a source for gathering puzzle pieces. Accessing the Spirit through prayer can open spiritual lines of communication that can bless our lives with understanding and wisdom. Those communications are indispensable if we wish move away from the waterfall and into the peaceful waters of safety.

Aha moments, those times when the eyes of our understanding are opened, can provide benchmarks of our recovery. We progress though a series of such moments as we move upstream. Each one moves us further away from acting out and closer to Him and recovery. However much you currently are praying, it is not enough. Pray constantly for his guidance and healing influence.

Elder Richard G. Scott was once anxious about his ability to convey to his audience his testimony and knowledge of the principles he wished to discuss with them. After wrestling with the issue he states:

Then a peace enveloped me. I felt that if I strive the best I can to talk with you, and you listen with an open mind and heart, with real intent, having faith in the Lord, then it won't matter too much what I say. You will have impressions come to you that will be individually tailored to your needs (Scott, 2001).

Those types of impressions are available to us in many settings. We must always keep our mind and heart open through humility and willingness. We must maintain real intent and commitment, and exercise our faith in the Lord. That qualifies us to receive the impressions we need for guidance and direction.

For those who have lost their membership in the Church, and, therefore, the Gift of the Holy Ghost, do not despair! Many believe that when we lose the Gift of the Holy Ghost, we lose access to spiritual inspiration. Do not underestimate the Light of Christ *that lighteth every man that cometh into the world* (John 1:9).

As President Eyring reminds us:

Every child of Heavenly Father born in the world is given, as a free gift, the Light of Christ. You have felt that. It is the sense of what is right and what is wrong and what is true and what is false. That has been with you since your journey in life began.

President Eyring goes on quote Moroni:

For behold, the Spirit of Christ is given to every man, that he may know good from evil; wherefore, I show unto you the way to judge; for every thing which inviteth to do good, and to persuade to believe in Christ, is sent forth by the power and gift of Christ; wherefore ye may know with a perfect knowledge it is of God.

But whatsoever thing persuadeth men to do evil, and believe not in Christ, and deny him, and serve not God, then ye may know with a perfect knowledge it is of the devil; for after this manner doth the devil work, for he persuadeth no man to do good, no, not one; neither do his angels; neither do they who subject themselves unto him (Eyring, 2008).

The Light of Christ is a very powerful tool for accessing the inspirations and teachings of the Spirit of the Lord. Cultivate it. Strengthen it by prayer and fasting. Learn to recognize its voice in your life.

Establish and maintain sobriety.

Establishing sobriety is the beginning point of recovery. The things we do up to that point are really preparatory for recovery. This is where the recovery process starts. It has already been designated for you as Mile 0 on the Recovery Highway. Sobriety eases the power of our addictive-thinking errors. We begin to see things quite differently from the vantage point of sobriety. That is why we establish and maintain sobriety.

> *Angelo was a new member of our recovery group. We were all working on some sort of recovery from sexual addiction. Angelo was a porn guy. As he told his story, it was obvious that being here wasn't his idea. His wife was upset by his viewing porn and demanded that he attend the group. He finished telling his story by saying,*
>
> *"I only do it once or twice a week, I don't think I really have a problem."*
>
> *The group leader wisely asked Angelo, "Does your wife think once or twice a week is not a problem? Or, how about your Priest, (Angelo being Catholic) does he think that isn't problem?"*
>
> *Angelo didn't answer, but he kept coming back. A few months later, he was able to laugh at himself for his statements on his first night, and he was often reminded of them by his friends at group. They did so not to embarrass him but to remind him and all of us present how much differently we see things when sobriety gets established.*

The White Book says this about sobriety: *Everything begins with sobriety. Without sobriety there is no program of recovery. But without reversing the deadly traits that underline our addiction, there is no positive and lasting sobriety* (Sexaholics Anonymous, 2002).

Establish a sobriety date. It is the day from which we will no longer act out. This draws your line in the sand. Vow never to cross it again. Mark it on your calendar. Count each day that you achieve sobriety beyond that date. Celebrate the anniversaries. Make keeping your sobriety your purpose. Defend and maintain your sobriety because, without it, you are in your addiction. Without it, you are an addict.

Just establishing sobriety is not enough. We must also begin finding a way to *reverse the deadly traits that underline our addiction* so we can have positive and lasting sobriety that leads to healing.

When companies fall into financial trouble and are in danger of failing, they often hire a turnaround specialist, a hired gun that can fix the problems. They begin by stopping the hemorrhaging, getting cash flow under control so that the company can survive. Then attention can be given to long term solutions to ensure the companies' future viabilities.

In recovery, establishing sobriety stops the bleeding and allows recovery to begin. We also need to begin resolving underlying issues to gain long term viability for our sobriety.

That would mean we need to figure out not only what got us to addiction in the first place, but also what keeps us there. Often, we need the help of trained professionals to sort out some of the details. Therapists who have successfully worked with others can be a great tool for your recovery. They have seen individuals struggle with problems very similar to your own. So, working with such a therapist can provide you with a shortcut to some of your recovery solutions.

Some believe that they are no longer addicts because they equate achieving sobriety with the idea that they have recovered. They turn a blind eye to those underlying issues and other addictive behaviors in their lives.

Sobriety and recovery are not synonymous. They are quite different. There are many in the recovery community, who hold a great deal of

sobriety, but have very little recovery. They are still trapped in their addictive behaviors and thinking errors. While they do abstain from their
drug of choice, the serenity of recovery continues to elude them.

Elder Bruce C. Hafen puts it this way:

*Some people want to keep one hand on the wall of the temple while
touching the world's unclean things with the other hand. We must put both
hands on the temple and hold on for dear life. One hand is not even almost
enough* (Hafen, 2004).

Serenity is the fruit of maintaining sobriety, which means doing the
work of recovery and moving closer to Christ. It is the peace that comes
with healing. Serenity is a sign that real recovery and healing is taking
place. Its coming de-marks moving from the Discovery Phase to the Recovery Phase in our healing process. We are no longer just abstaining;
we are healing.

Keep a Recovery Journal

If I could give someone in search of recovery only one tool, it would be
a Recovery Journal. Something as simple as a composition notebook
works very well. A Recovery Journal serves several purposes. It can be
the outlet for feelings and emotions. It can be the chronicle of "Aha"
or healing moments. It can be a collection of quotes from speakers or
books, verses of scripture or personal impressions that have had special
impact during the healing process. For anyone in recovery, a Recovery
Journal will, in time, become a great resource.

Erin talks of her Recovery Journal:

> *Boy, it has saved my bacon more than once. I read it
> whenever I get discouraged or feel tempted to act out. It
> reminds me of how far I have come and of what I have
> learned. It helps me remember I don't want to go back
> there. I find encouragement by reading it; it provides inspi-
> ration, new motivation and courage, usually when I need
> them the most. I cannot count the times that I have written*

a verse or quote that really gave me hope or understanding or strength and, when I go back to it weeks or months later, it reinvigorates me again. It is like a never-ending wellspring of healing influence for me.

Jill says of her Recovery Journal:

I write in mine all the time. Sometimes it is just about how I am feeling or the struggle I am having. I always feel better for doing it. Then there are the times when I go on my binges and look up everything I can find on a certain subject, like deliverance, or faith, and record what I find. It has become my recovery file cabinet. I keep my recovery resources there and refer to them often.

The most important part of having a Recovery Journal is using it. Keep it with you and record in it often. Record your successes, your struggles, your moments of inspiration and your times of healing. The body of your recovery work, recorded in a journal, will be a treasure chest of future strength and further healing for you. The quotes, scriptures and ideas that have inspired you in the past can be harvested over and over for new inspiration and strength. As you heal and your understanding grows, you will find completely new insights and directions whenever you return to your journal. Over time, they can take on a personally sacred standing with us.

Ron says:

I don't know how many times I have turned the pages in my Journal and rediscovered the inspirations that I needed. There is great power in bringing those inspirational moments back into my consciousness. Ether 12:27 is one that has helped me repeatedly. As I have pondered, "I give unto men weakness..." my insights have grown with

*my understanding. I have found comfort and encourage-
ment there countless times.*

Find Your Feelings. Reconnect With Your Emotional Self.

*WHAT? Why is it always about feelings with you therapists? What is so
stinking important about feelings?* (Bryan, at the time, was not a very successful recovering addict.)

A major outcome of addiction is that it cuts us off from our feelings.
We begin to lose touch with them when we begin isolating ourselves in
order to use our drug of choice. The loss is completed as we build the
emotional bonds between our feelings and acting out. Eventually, the
response for every feeling and emotion might be translated to an urge
to use our drug of choice. The feeling is so connected to the urge, and
the effect so immediate, that we lose our ability to distinguish what the
originating feeling was. We don't bother trying to understand the message of our feelings, it is always the same, *I need to use.* The result is we
lose contact with our emotional self.

In a scene that has been repeated many times, clients new to recovery respond to the question, "What are you feeling?" with a look of con-
sternation as they realize that they neither recognize, nor can verbalize,
what they are feeling! *If you are like most addicts, you are unaware of parts
of yourself, including your feelings. Without that self-knowledge, you misper-
ceive your own reality* (Carnes, 1994). Our feelings and emotions have a
great guiding purpose in our life, if we lose contact with them or *misper-
ceive* them we get lost quickly.

Our feelings provide feedback that keeps us connected with ourselves and others, including our Heavenly Father. When we are able to
use the messages and wisdom of our emotions by experiencing them
properly, we gain valuable guidance for our thinking, decision-making and actions. We become successful at things like loving and being
loved, one of our most basic human needs. Unpleasant feelings guide
us to make improvements in our behavior, such as when we feel guilt
from taking advantage of a friend. Pleasant feelings guide us by bringing

calmness, peace, and increased self-esteem that reinforce and encourage healthy behaviors.

In our addiction, we short circuit our emotional system and stop listening to the messages of our feelings. The peace and reinforcing powers of healthy behaviors, those very vital *to self* messages, get silenced. Without that guidance we begin to distance ourselves from the sources of emotional strength—our family, friends and the Savior.

Regaining contact with our feelings begins with regaining the ability to identify our emotions and decode the signals that they are sending us. Then we need to observe and use the direction and guidance that they provide for our thinking and problem solving. It is also important that we gain an understanding of the underlying sources of our emotions. These underlying issues may be areas that need our attention. When we become proficient in the management of our emotions, we will be able to use their input in our reasoning, problem solving, judgments and behaviors. All emotions bring us information; those we enjoy feeling and those we dread all have their place in our processing.

We begin to reconnect with our feelings by first gaining sobriety. Sobriety is an absolutely critical step. We will not make progress without it. Reuniting with our feelings cannot take place while we are still participating in our addiction. When sobriety becomes established, we can begin the process of rediscovering our emotional selves. In some ways, it is like learning a new language. We have lost (or never had) the ability to translate the messages imbedded in our feelings. When our feelings speak to us, we only hear a confusing gibberish that we recognize as the urge to use, and we can't translate those messages to our understanding for the direction we need. When we start to learn the art of translating the messages of our emotions and feelings, we begin to reconnect with our emotional self.

Start emotional reconnecting with the simple practice of asking yourself, several times a day: *What am I feeling right now?* Try to verbalize your feelings, to yourself and to others. Verbally describing what we feel helps reestablish our conscious contact with our emotional self. Reviewing our interactions with others can be instructive by asking the following: *What did I feel? How emotional was I? Did I accurately express my feelings? What could I have done better?*

Use the following list of *feeling words* to increase your translation skills. Review the list often. Recognize the feelings that you are experiencing or those you have felt recently. If you find *feeling words* that you think you have never experienced, try to imagine what that feeling would be like. Do a little experimenting and exploring and begin to reconnect and expand your emotional vocabulary.

abandoned	desirous	happy	nutty	sneaky
adequate	despairing	hassled	obnoxious	solemn
adamant	destructive	hate	obsessed	sorrowful
affectionate	determined	heavenly	odd	spiteful
agonized	diffident	helpful	opposed	startled
almighty	diminished	helpless	outraged	stingy
ambivalent	distracted	high	overwhelmed	stuffed
annoyed	distraught	homesick	pain	stupid
anxious	disturbed	honored	panicked	stunned
apathetic	dominated	hurt	peaceful	stupefied
astounded	divided	hysterical	persecuted	suffering
awed	dubious	ignored	petrified	sure
bad	eager	immortal	pity	sympathetic
beautiful	ecstatic	impressed	pleasant	talkative
betrayed	electrified	infatuated	pleased	tempted
bitter	empty	infuriated	precarious	tenacious
blissful	enchanted	inspired	pretty	tenuous
bold	energetic	intimidated	prim	tense
brave	envious	isolated	prissy	tentative
burdened	excited	jealous	proud	terrible
calm	evil	joyous	quarrelsome	terrified
capable	exasperated	jumpy	rage	tested

captivated	exhausted	kind	rapture	tired
challenged	fascinated	keen	refreshed	thwarted
charmed	fawning	laconic	rejected	troubled
cheated	fearful	lazy	relieved	ugly
cheerful	flustered	lecherous	relaxed	uneasy
childish	foolish	left out	remorse	unsettled
clever	fragmented	licentious	restless	violent
combative	frazzled	lonely	reverent	vehement
competitive	frustrated	longing	rewarded	vital
condemned	frightened	love	righteous	vulnerable
confused	full	low	sad	victorious
conspicuous	furious	mad	satisfied	vexed
contented	glad	maudlin	scared	vivacious
contrite	good	mean	screwed up	wicked
cruel	gratified	melancholy	servile	wonderful
crushed	greedy	miserable	settled	weepy
culpable	grief	mystical	sexy	wild
deceitful	groovy	naughty	shocked	worried
defeated	guilty	nervous	silly	zany
delighted	gullible	nice	skeptical	zapped

There are two things to keep in mind about feelings: They cannot be ignored, and they cannot be in control of our lives. If we are experiencing either of these extremes, we are in trouble. We often think we can hide our feelings, but we are not very good at that either.

We must learn to experience and process our emotions and feelings in such a way that we can again receive their guiding influence in our lives. Using the following questions can help us harvest the wisdom and guidance of our emotions:

1. What am I feeling right now? What is this coming from?

2. What is this feeling trying to tell me? What wisdom can I gain from this?

3. What do I need to do with this information? What do I need? (O'Malley, 2004).

Move from your emotionally based decision-making process to a spiritually based decision-making process.

The addict's mantra is *I want what I want, when I want it!* The addict's decision-making process is driven by it. It is a decision-making process based on emotion. It results in the continual response of behavior that is based on placating self. As addicts, we consider only ourselves. We get lost in ourselves and our selfishness. Heavenly Father had a different model in mind for us.

In this life, we have to make many choices. Some are very important choices. Some are not. Many of our choices are between good and evil. The choices we make, however, determine to a large extent our happiness or our unhappiness, because we have to live with the consequences of our choices. Making perfect choices all of the time is not possible. It just doesn't happen. But it is possible to make good choices we can live with and grow from. When God's children live worthy of divine guidance they can become "free forever, knowing good from evil; to act for themselves and not to be acted upon" (James E. Faust, 2004).

Moving to a spiritually based decision-making process can help us make *choices we can live with and grow from* so we can avoid the difficult consequences of addiction. This is what Nephi meant when he said *free forever...to act for themselves and not to be acted upon.*

President Ezra Taft Benson gave us an excellent example of what a spiritually based decision-making process would look like. He suggested that we use the following six questions as a guide in decision-making:

1. *Is it contrary to the revealed will or commandments of God?*

2. *Could it harm any individual, family, or group?*

83

3. *Would the decision make* [me] *a better person?*

4. *Could it retard or injure spiritual or moral growth?*

5. *Could it create unhappy or unpeaceful memories?*

6. *Could a blessing be derived from this particular action?* (The LDS Woman, 2000).

Elder Boyd K. Packer suggests additional ways that can help us in establishing a spiritually based decision-making process, especially when we are using that process to make major decisions: *Work it out in your own mind first. Ponder on it and analyze it and meditate on it. Read the scriptures. Pray about it. I've come to learn that major decisions can't be forced. You must look ahead and have vision. Ponder on things a little each day...measure the problem against what you know to be right and wrong and then make a decision. Then ask Him if the decision is right or if it is wrong* (Packer, 1975).

Making this change in how we process decisions is a critical step. This falls into the *change everything we can that might be part of the problem* category suggested by Elder Jeffrey R. Holland (Holland, 2006). It allows us to move away from selfishness and into accountability and will result in a significant shift in behavior.

Become ridiculously accountable.

I could never figure out why knowing the truth about God never set me free. Or the truth about psychology or the Twelve-Step program. But when I finally came to the place where I saw the truth about me—and despaired... Well, that was the beginning...The truth about ourselves, becomes the raw material from which our new lives are built (Sexaholics Anonymous, 2002).

When I saw the truth about me—and despaired. Recovery is established and maintained by being accountable, ridiculously accountable. Accountability can eliminate secrecy, isolation and the selfishness that addiction thrives on. They provide the freedom to act out and they are the stage for the addiction play.

Drug addicts are always in stealth mode, hiding from the law. Porn addicts need secrecy and privacy to engage, so they constantly are hiding from the awareness of their spouse or others. It is not unusual for alcoholics to drink alone, taking great lengths to hide the purchase, consumption, and disposition of empty bottles. Isolation and secrecy are the breeding grounds for acting out. Accountability is the antidote we spray on those grounds to eradicate them.

Support groups are tremendous assets in establishing accountability. In a support group, we find a nonjudgmental group of our peers who have understanding and compassion about our struggle. Our confessions are not burdens to them. We can and should be accountable with our sobriety and behaviors in this setting. We learned that making a confession killed the secrets that gave our addiction life. Support groups are the places to keep our lives free of new secrets that might impede our recovery.

We must establish other ways of being held accountable as well. For example, Internet porn users find programs that log site activities for others to see to be very useful in precluding acting out. Frequent check-ins, where we can report what is currently going on for us, can also be very helpful. Bishops, sponsors, therapists and other trusted individuals can serve as accountability partners with good results.

Spouses are not good candidates for accountability partners. While we must be accountable to our spouse to uphold our promises and commitments to them; moment-to-moment accountability often puts more stress on them than they deserve. Remember, you are responsible for your recovery, not them. Out of respect for the damage and suffering that your addictive behaviors have already caused, you should not put them in a position that they might feel in any way responsible for your healing.

A truly difficult part of recovery is understanding the damage that we have caused others, especially our spouses. If we are selfish enough to engage in an addiction, we probably aren't the most compassionate, understanding and comforting spouse to begin with. As we begin to heal, we feel the old burdens drop, and we move forward. We begin to feel the happiness of recovery long before those around us. As for the spouse, he or she often lag behind. Your old burdens are new to your spouse, and they are still trying to process them. Your spouse's world has been rocked if your addiction is a new revelation. Respect the struggle he or she are in.

Consider being accountable to your spouse on a round-by-round basis rather than a blow-by-blow basis. Boxing matches are scored by the round, the ups and downs of each fighter considered in the scoring over three minutes. Blow-by-blow accountability to your spouse can be confusing and discouraging. The meaning of the ups and downs of recovery is difficult to understand and responses are often very heightened. The highs lead to the euphoria of believing the battle is over and downs to the devastating belief that it will never be done. The mood swings between the two can be overwhelming.

Dr. Doug Weiss, in his Heart to Heart Counseling Center for treatment of sexual addictions, uses an unusual form of accountability. Addicts in the program purchase a lie detector test gift card and present it to their spouses with the commitment to submit at the spouse's request to the test. This becomes a powerful deterrent. Any hope for secrecy or not being held accountable has been eliminated. Even just the awareness of the possibility of accountability destroys the stage to act out upon.

Begin a quest to find serenity, a benchmark of recovery.

Our next goal is to find serenity. Serenity is the change in our lives that tells us that our recovery work has not been in vain. Sometimes it is easier to describe what serenity is not. When we are in our addiction, our lives have a chaotic feel, and we might experience torment, despair, loss of control, fear, anger, self-hatred, frustration, disappointment, isolation, selfishness, loneliness, anxiety or depression. Serenity is the absence of those emotions and manifests as that sweet, calming influence, that gentle, kind spirit, that profound feeling of peace and comfort, the knowledge that all is well, the very feeling of the pure love of Christ, directed by Him, to us.

A new heart...will I give you, a new spirit will I put within you: and I will take away the stony heart out of your flesh (Ezekial 36:26). That *new heart,* that *new spirit* is the phenomenon we call serenity. It is the presence of the Spirit in our lives. It is the sense that we are in conscious contact with our Savior.

Ron tells this story:

> *I once worked on a construction project near the Arctic Circle in Alaska. The modest cabin that housed the workers had a rather large and noisy diesel generator that sat very close to the cabin's sidewall. The noise and vibration were heard and felt constantly. One night as we lay sleeping it ran out of fuel. When I awoke the silence and calm mystified me. I knew something was very different but could not put my finger on what had changed. A coworker arose and immediately announced that the generator had stopped. My mystery was solved, and I was left to contemplate the comfort and peace of the silence that was in such contrast to the noise and distraction of the running generator.*

Finding serenity is a very similar experience. After we have learned to practice sobriety and have successfully begun the work of recovery, we may be *mystified* by the sudden appearance of serenity's peace and comfort. We notice the obvious disappearance of chaos in our lives.

One addict took several days to recognize that the new sense of calm and peace in his life was serenity. He felt out of place, as if he was traveling in a foreign country, because there was an oddness to it, and he was a stranger to these newfound feelings. This is the peace that comes from recovery. This is the peace that comes from change and healing. Its arrival is a benchmark in the recovery process.

The Big Book promises that as we work the steps, *we will comprehend the word serenity and we will know peace* (Bill W., 84). Serenity isn't something we can preview or learn from a teacher. We understand serenity by getting there. We comprehend the word by achieving it. You will know it when you get there.

There is a glorious miracle awaiting every soul who is prepared to change

...when lives are changed—then comes the great miracle to beautify and warm and lift...it brings peace to the previously anxious, restless, frustrated, perhaps tormented soul (Kimball, 2006). These are also the descriptors of serenity. Make no mistake about the path we follow; we may call it recovery at times, but the road we are on is the path of repentance that leads to forgiveness. We seek the Savior's healing touch. We seek the serenity that comes with that connection to Him.

Once we have found serenity, we are not done. We have just gotten started, but the coming of serenity verifies that we are on the right path, and that we are doing the right things. We now can set our goal for *the mighty change of heart* (Alma 5:14) that is the fruit of recovery work.

Remember AA's promise quoted earlier: *If we are painstaking about this phase of our development, we will be amazed before we are half way through. We are going to know a new freedom and a new happiness. We will comprehend the word serenity and we will know peace. Our whole attitude and outlook upon life will change. We will intuitively know how to handle situations which used to baffle us. We will suddenly realize that God is doing for us what we could not do for ourselves.*

Are these extravagant promises? We think not. They are being fulfilled among us—sometimes quickly, sometimes slowly. They will always materialize if we work for them.

Putting Tools in Your Tool Kit

Now that we know the rules, it is time to add some tools to our recovery toolkit so we can keep the rules. This is about skill building. We have to get better at doing the work. We need to move from being an apprentice to becoming a journeyman in recovery. Later we will gather some advanced tools to help us move to the master skill level, but we really need to become expert with the following tools first. In most recovery situations we will use a combination of skills to protect ourselves and continue healing. Because our approach to recovery is Christ-centered, our efforts always include Him. Prayer, fasting and reading the scriptures are givens, these are additional tools for our use.

Turn It Over

Our most powerful and versatile tool is our ability to *turn it over*. It should be the first one we reach for. Turning It Over is the continued observance of Early Recovery Rule #6, *turning our mind and will over to the Savior for His care and keeping.* When struggles challenge our recovery we turn them over to our Savior. We might say:

Lord I am feeling challenged by this urge to use, if I keep thinking about it, I might relapse, I am going to turn it over to you.

Ron learned the skill this way:

> *The day I learned to turn it over was quite a day. Part of my acting out sexually was elaborate planning. Just thinking about how and when I was going to act out. I used to think it was just harmless fun until I realized it was part of my acting out ritual. It was the beginning of the cycle for me. I really fixated on making my plans and wouldn't think about anything else. I couldn't turn it off. As I began my recovery and learned about turning it over, I decided that next time I started one of my planning binges, I would turn it over. I was pretty excited to have a defense mechanism.*
>
> *At the time, I had an hour long drive to work. The downtime of the drive had often been spent in one of my binges, and as I pulled out of my driveway, I started in. My mind knew the drill and went from 0 to 60 in no time. I thought I was ready with my new tool. I turned it over.*
>
> *Dear Lord if I think about this, I will act out, so I am going to turn this over to you.*
>
> *Immediately I felt some relief and calming. I was very proud of myself for about 30 seconds, when I realized my planning binge was back.*
>
> *I turned it over. It came back.*
>
> *I turned it over. It came back.*
>
> *I turned on some very spiritual music. I turned my struggle over. It came back.*

I turned up the music and turned it over. It came back.

I really turned up the music and turned it over. It came back.

I started singing at the top of my lungs with the music and turned it over. It came back. And so my struggle ensued for nearly an hour. I was in tears and feeling very drained as I neared my destination, but I realized that the binge had finally stopped coming back. I guess my addict just wanted to know if I was serious.

Ever since that day, when I turn things over, they usually stay turned over. Sometimes I may have to do it a couple of times, but when I do get it turned over, I am done with it.

Turning it over works for more than just troublesome thoughts. Emotions that challenge us can also be turned over. Anxiety, depression and other emotions can be turned over and left behind. Like Ron's experience, it may take some persistence, but if we muster the effort, the challenging thoughts and emotions will leave us.

Turning it over is also an indication that we are giving up our need to be in control, which is a further indication of our submission to Him. We are taking Him up on His invitation to *Come unto me, all ye that labour and are heavy laden, and I will give you rest* (Matt 11:28). A way that we receive that *rest* from our burdens is by turning them over to Him.

Healthy Self-Talk

Self-talk is that constant inner chatter or dialogue that we have with ourselves, Healthy self-talk can be a valuable tool for recovery. Conversely, the existence of negative self-talk can devastate any recovery effort we might mount.

Mary's self-talk was dominated by, "I am such an idiot!" and other very negative comments. She never was quite good enough, always finding some flaw or mistake in every part of her life. Mary struggled with relationships and a sexual addiction. She loved being in love, especially the romantic, falling in love stage. A very attractive woman, she, nevertheless, thought of herself as lacking and became afraid and angry at any signal that her partner was disappointed or pulling away from her. She knew she wasn't good enough—her self-talk confirmed it regularly, but she reacted poorly when she felt her partner was beginning to believe it.

Mary was so defensive that totally innocuous remarks were often perceived as statements that she, yet again, was not good enough. The most innocent of events would set her off in torrid emotional storms. Mary never suffered alone. She always took it out on whomever was unlucky enough to be around at the moment. Her relationships oscillated from intensely close and romantic enmeshment, to volatile arguments and estrangement. Mary, it seemed, was euphoric one day, so in love and happy, then completely out of love and overwhelmed by depression, fear and anxiety the next.

Mary's self-talk was a big factor and was, in part, killing any chance for a successful relationship and happiness.

You talk to yourself constantly ... and you become the architect and creator of the emotions you later experience through this self-talk.

Emotions do not come as the result of an observation or an experience but rather as the result of the things we say to ourselves about those ... situations. Thus two people can have the same experience or observe the same event and come away with very different conclusions and emotions (Sorensen, 1998).

Mary's anxiety and depression were a direct result of her negative (*I am such an idiot*) inner chatter. As she repeated such statements to herself countless times, she came to accept it as true and its attendant emotions, self-hatred, depression and anxiety came with that decision. Those emotions always lie just below the surface for her and are easily made active by the slightest provocation in her relationship.

Low self-esteem is a low pressure system around which the emotional storms of our lives form. It helps to learn skills to combat and manage fear, anxiety, depression, anger and the other emotions, but if we can eliminate the low pressure system of low self-esteem, those emotional storms have great difficulty forming.

Anger can lead us to feel or say unkind things to or about others. [and ourselves] *Christ specifically warned against using such words as fool or raca, terms of contempt or derision in both Greek and Aramaic* (Matthew 5:22). *Today, other words may be more common—like stupid or idiot. But the principle is the same. Whether we use these terms in anger or in making fun of someone* [or ourselves] *such behavior is inconsistent with the gospel view of the worth of souls.*

Anger is spiritually damaging to all concerned but especially so to the offender, who is in danger of [God's] *judgment, the council and hellfire* (Dahl 1999). If that threat of spiritual danger exists for us as we feel and express anger to and about others, so also it must apply as we turn our anger inward and use damaging and hateful self-talk. We are expressing contempt for the worth of our very own soul. When we do that, we definitely are not on the same page as the Savior.

Sometimes we fall into the trap of believing that being hard on ourselves, *yelling at ourselves,* if you will, is just a way of holding ourselves accountable or motivating ourselves to better behaviors. We come to believe that our negative tongue lashings have some positive result, and by beating ourselves up, we increase our desire to change and be better. That does not happen. Instead, love, praise, understanding and the elements of compassion are the foundations of personal change and growth. Self-hatred and self-punishment stifle growth and keep us in self-destructive behaviors. We must move away from them to heal.

Each time we use hurtful self-talk, a harmful emotional residue is created. The effect is miniscule at first, but, when negative self-talk is repeated habitually, the damage becomes significant. The feelings generated from what accumulates cannot be ignored. They are factored into our decision-making process.

Just as our body reacts to every experience with feelings and emotions, it reacts to our self-talk. Our emotional center cannot distinguish between current real life events and the events of the past that we relive in our mind, nor can it discern that self-talk is not from the outside world but our own inner voice.

The emotional center does not pass judgment or consider the source. Its job is to react and provide an appropriate feeling or emotion for the event on main stage of the brain. It always does its job, creating the feeling and emotions called for. The problem comes when we constantly feed the system negative self-talk or relive embarrassing experiences over and over. The redundant negative memories and self-talk are treated just like new incoming messages from the real world.

When we repeat that we are a stupid idiot countless times, countless layers of harmful feelings of disappointment and self-hatred are laid down. The residue grows with each event. It eventually assumes a life of its own. We become ashamed, certain we are damaged and unworthy of anything good. We even take on self-destructive behaviors to self-sabotage to prove our point.

We accomplish the same kind of destructive results by reliving over and over in our mind our moments of perceived failure. The emotional center treats each reliving as a new real time, real world event. When we relive our failure a thousand times in our imagination, a thousand residues of shame are laid down. The emotional center thinks we have failed a thousand times, and not just once. The emotional residue created of a thousand perceived failures can become an overwhelming burden.

Because love, praise, understanding and the elements of compassion are the foundations upon which humans are able to make changes and grow, our self-talk should take on a wise, compassionate and forgiving tone. These positive self-talk tracks, laid down a thousand times, can build layers of confidence and self-love that will strengthen and heal us.

After a disappointing performance we might say: *That didn't go very well. I wish that had gone better. Next time I will work and prepare to do a better job.*

When things go badly and we are disappointed: *That wasn't the outcome I wanted. This wasn't my day. We all have those kinds of days. Next time things may turn out differently.*

When we embarrass ourselves: *I can't believe I did that. Sometimes I do silly things. I am learning that everyone does. It is part of being human. I am going to try to learn from this.*

When someone lets us down: *Wow, what a surprise that was, I didn't think he would do that. I know we all make mistakes, I know he was doing the best he could. Sometimes, because we are human, our best isn't very good.*

When we are trying to recover from addiction: *I have suffered a lot for some of my choices. Some parts of my life are a real mess. I am on the right path now. Things are getting better. I just need to keep doing my recovery work.*

When we find ourselves excommunicated: *I never thought I would end up here. I am getting to face some difficult consequences for my choices. This will be very hard to endure, but I know that I can. I know it will help me heal. I am going to make the most of this time to rebuild and heal myself and reach out to the Savior.*

When we fail: *Boy I really biffed this time. I now know that failures are a part of life. Everyone experiences them. Successful people learn and grow from them. This hurts a lot, but I can learn from this. I will be okay.*

Sorenson makes some further helpful points to remember for our self-talk:

Everyone makes mistakes. Making a mistake does not mean you are inadequate or incompetent.

Everyone does things they later regret.

Everyone has embarrassing moments.

Others are not as aware of what you say or do as you are. They are usually focused on their own concerns.

Being likable does not mean that everyone will like you.

Everyone experiences rejection, whether in job interviews, possible romantic relationships, or simply by insensitive people.

Everyone experiences disapproval. You can't please everyone all the time.

Being imperfect is not synonymous with being inadequate. No one is perfect!

(Sorensen, 1998).

Celebrating Your Sobriety Date

By remembering and celebrating our sobriety date, we keep our focus on recovery. We are reminded often of how far we have come and of what we have accomplished. We also are reminded that our addiction is only a slip or two away. It helps us set goals for future sobriety. AA and the groups that are patterned on the Twelve Step model present coins to mark time in sobriety.

> *When I got my six-month coin, I was pretty stoked. That was the first time I allowed myself to think that I really might make it this time. I kept that coin on me always, in my front pocket. I enjoyed rubbing it, and slipping it through my fingers. When I had an acting out thought or urge, I went for my coin. It comforted me and it gave me new strength. I didn't want to go back to my old life, but I had failed so many times. I often lost confidence and started to fear for my recovery. The coin in my pocket helped me remember that I didn't need to fail again.*

That is how Ron used his coin to keep himself safe. He was defending his sobriety, trying to keep it alive and trying to extend it.

Sobriety anniversaries give us a chance to celebrate our accomplishments. Not so much in the spirit of celebration but in the spirit of gratitude—gratitude for healing and for change, gratitude for Him and His plan, gratitude for His love for us and our feeble success at making our way to Him.

Look Away! Look Away!

Look Away! is the simplest and most powerful tool we can put in our recovery toolkit. It keeps us out of trouble and it puts down anchor in the safe Waters of Recovery, away from the waters that pull us towards the falls of acting out. A big part of look away is the act of avoiding the looking at or thinking about anything that might entice us towards our addictive behaviors. We must look away with more than just our eyes.

We cannot be physically present with reminders of our addiction, nor can we tolerate thoughts that put us in an addiction fantasy. We must look away by not hanging out in old haunts where we acted out. We must look away by not hanging out with old user friends. We must look away by not fondly remembering the good old days and romanticizing them in our memories. We cannot afford to give place to such thoughts or behaviors, because they will betray our recovery. It is not enough to just stop acting out; we must also eliminate these supporting behaviors that are part of our addictive lifestyle.

Those affected by sexual addictions can especially benefit from the look away tool. Sex addicts become very proficient at taking hits. The alcoholic has to go and buy some alcohol before he can participate in his addiction. The meth or marijuana guy has to go and buy some product before they can hit the bong or indulge. Sex addict guy is carrying around his drug of choice in his brain. He has become very good at releasing those feel-good brain chemicals. He need buy no drug, nor does he need to find a partner to act out with. The sex addict can make the brain give him a hit by looking at a provocative scene, or just by looking at a not so provocative scene and wondering, *What if?* He can even get a hit just by remembering and mentally reliving old exploits.

The addict learns to generate sexual thoughts that will release his drug of choice, the neurotransmitters involved in sexual arousal, in his brain. He becomes so expert that not much outside influence is needed. What might be a very provocative scene to a sex addict might go completely unnoticed by a non-addict.

A telltale sign of some sex addicts is that they sexualize their lives to the point that it constantly surfaces in conversation. They find the sexual overtones in even innocent conversation or events. It is their way of keeping the flow of arousal chemicals going in the brain. They become constant users. Others are unaware and even amused at the addict's ability to make sexual jokes. We might not even find the addict's behavior vulgar or improper, just naughty humor, almost appearing innocent.

Unfortunately, if we are really being accountable, it isn't possible to be almost innocent of acting out.

Continuing to take hits even after starting recovery can be a huge roadblock, and those who do so have lost the Recovery Attitude of Accountability. Outwardly the addict's constant sexualization of the world is unseen. This form of his acting out can remain secret. Others might assume recovery is underway. Even the addict might not be able to recognize what he is doing to himself. He may have been sexualizing things for a very long time, and it feels normal. It seems far removed from looking at porn or having an affair or any other way of sexually acting out.

"Hey, I am not having sex with anyone; I am not acting out," he might rationalize. It is easily justified. "Boys will be boys," we say or, "You can look but not touch." All this time he doesn't realize this constant sexualization gets in the way of recovery. We are still using. It blocks our spiritual connection. We cannot access the Savior, and serenity cannot arrive.

Allowing sexually stimulating memories or fantasies to have a place in our mind can also derail recovery. *In a world saturated with immoral aural and visual stimuli, such thoughts and temptations* [to act out sexually] *can be daily fare.*

Although we cannot avoid the stimuli, we can plead with the Lord to help us control and channel our thoughts. We can consciously avoid compromising situations and forthrightly resist temptation. Rather than allowing improper thoughts to linger—and enhancing and savoring them—we can dismiss them [Look Away!]*...and deliberately channel our thoughts into positive paths.*

If we imagine ourselves involved in improper things, our thoughts may influence our heart's inclination and perhaps even our future behavior. Dr. Maxwell Maltz underscores the connection between our thoughts and our body's nervous system: "Experimental and clinical psychologists have proved beyond a shadow of a doubt that the human nervous system cannot tell the difference between an 'actual' experience and an experience imagined vividly and in detail" (Dahl 1991).

The Lord's directive is *that you would humble yourselves before the*

Lord and call on His holy name. And watch and pray continually that ye may not be tempted above that which ye can bear (Alma 13:28). We can accomplish this by not harboring or giving place to thoughts and imaginings that sexually arouse. And it applies to all addicts, for any thoughts that arise that remind us fondly of our acting out. We must dispute them when they appear. James promises that if *we resist the devil...he will flee from* [us] (Dahl, 1991). When we learn to send using thoughts away by turning them over, and avoid them by looking away, we will have made a huge step toward humbling ourselves before the Lord.

The 500-Pound Telephone

The 500-pound telephone tool is hard for many to use. Everyone has it in their toolbox, but it often just lies around gathering dust. People seem to be afraid of using it. Its nonuse is certainly not because they do not know how it works. We dial the phone all day long, except, it seems, when we move into addict mode.

When a client appears on my doorstep, with discouragement on his face, and makes confession of a relapse, we discuss the sequence of events that led to acting out. What was the genealogy of this slip? Step by step, we follow the events that led back to acting out. We try to find the headwaters of the behavior so that we can gain understanding of how our addict operates.

In such discussions, I will ask: *As all this was happening, did you call anyone?*

Invariably, the answer is: *No.*

One client, convicted by himself of his failure to call said, *Sometimes that telephone weighs 500 pounds I just can't pick it up.*

Mary explained her dilemma this way:

> *It seems like everyone that has been part of my life has hurt me in one way or another. It is really hard to not remember that and just freely trust others. I have had about all the hurt my life can handle; thank you, very much!*

When I do ask for help it feels like lose; lose. If someone does help me, I feel guilty for needing the help, and if they refuse me, I feel humiliated and very alone.

Fear and shame make the telephone heavy. Fear of how others will judge us and shame that we are struggling, yet again. Our addict loves his isolation, the false safety of thinking, "No one will know," also adds a few pounds to the weight of the phone. Many addicts, like Mary, struggle with trusting others, again adding to the heaviness.

One addict said: *I think it was easier to give up my alcohol than to pick up the phone.*

Early Recovery Rule #7 tells us to build a network of support. We should have a short list of friends or trusted confidants that we can call when we are struggling. When we are able to reach out and call someone, we combine the benefits of making confession and killing secrets with the Recovery Attitude of Accountability. That is a powerful recovery cocktail!

Ron talked about how the phone helps him:

You know, I have never met my recovery buddy, Scott. He lives 800 miles from here, but he has the same struggle that I do with sexual addiction. We met through a recovery Web site and have been e-mailing and telephoning ever since. I have lost count of the number of times I was struggling just a step away from acting out and I called Scott. When I tell him what I am dealing with, it suddenly loses its power over me. The temptation dissipates. And it works both ways. Scott calls and says: "I have got something to turn over to you, Ron." He tells me his story and the struggle ends for him. I'm not all that sure I know why it works. I just know that it does. When I am struggling and call Scott and share with him, the struggle goes away.

We can't always run to the therapist or access the Bishop. Others, like our sponsor, recovery buddies or members of our recovery group, can fill a valuable role in our recovery. We find relief by reaching out, ending isolation and sharing our struggle. The telephone is a very powerful tool if we can just pick it up and dial.

Mood Changers

It was our desire to change how we feel, or our mood, that brought us to addiction in the first place. Now we can use the same principle against our addiction as we recover. When we find ourselves edging downstream towards the falls and acting out, we can turn to a *Mood Changer* and get out of the grasp of our desire to act out. Develop a list of five behaviors and activities that significantly change your mood, that you can go to when you feel trouble coming on. Prayer and reading the scriptures are obvious, front line defenses that we should be implementing daily. Find five additional activities that work for you.

> *Bob had struggled with his addiction for nearly 35 years. He never got very far away from it. He had very little hope of recovering, "Maybe when I die," he would say in a very Eyore-like voice. Operating from this discouraged state, it took nearly three weeks, for him to come up with five activities that changed his mood.*
>
> 1. *Hunting with my dogs.*
> 2. *Working in the yard.*
> 3. *Taking a walk.*
> 4. *Helping someone else.*
> 5. *Watching my favorite movies.*
>
> *We modified "Hunting with my dogs" to "Playing, training, or hunting with my dogs," so that Bob could do it at almost anytime. We found a local homeless agency that needed drop-in volunteers, so Bob could help out whenever he was free or was feeling threatened. With the list*

complete, we made a contract that whenever he felt the addiction coming on, he would use one of his Mood Changers. I didn't see Bob for nearly a month after that. A very different Bob came back to see me. Eyore was gone, and Tigger had replaced him. "I can't believe the difference it makes!" he gushed. "I haven't acted out in a month, and it hasn't been that hard. I just go to a Mood Changer whenever I feel the addiction calling my name."

Exercise is an item almost everyone should put on their list. Whether it is walking, working out, bike riding, running, swimming or another form of exercise; when we exercise, a profound mood change can result. We use our brain to release feel good neurotransmitters that not only change our mood, but also strengthen and encourage us.

Priesthood blessings are also a mainstay as a Mood Changer. Ron tells the following story:

I was making plans and arrangements for some serious acting out that would have profound effects on my life. My home teacher knocked on my door because, he was in the neighborhood. After exchanging pleasantries, he asked, "Do you need a blessing?"

Because I was confused by his appearance at the time I was planning and preparing awful things, I stammered out a "No."

As we parted and I walked away, I became aware of how desperately I did need a blessing. I quickly found him, relieved that he was not already gone. He laid his hands on my head. I remember nothing of what he said, but that blessing changed my life. I walked away with only a desire to not act out. It not only changed my feelings and desires in that moment, but also it has helped me stay changed as I reflect back on that amazing experience.

Zero Tolerance

Our *Zero Tolerance* tool is really an attitude, an attitude of vigilance. Like the Nephites who built towers to watch for the attack of their enemies, we need to keep a vigilant eye on the approach of our addiction. We cannot tolerate even the smallest encroachment in our lives by our addictive behaviors. Zero Tolerance for addictive thoughts, feelings, or behaviors needs to be our mantra. We have other tools for counteracting the appearance of our addiction, but this tool keeps us consciously intent on what is happening inside of us and disputes the first sign of our addictive behaviors.

Rationalization and excuse making are the very fabric of addiction. Successful recovery can leave no place for them to exist in our lives.

It won't hurt anything. You deserve this. No one will know.

We need to dispute these kinds of thoughts and not give them place. In order to do that, we must be consciously aware of their appearance. It is easy to get lazy, not really aware of what we are thinking and float throughout the day on automatic pilot. Recovery demands a constant vigilance and a Zero Tolerance policy towards the existence of these kinds of thoughts.

Behavior Contract

Behavior Contracts are often used by parents or teachers in addressing problematic behaviors. These written agreements present in detail what the behavioral expectations are, and they outline the privileges and consequences that accompany meeting (or failing to meet) the terms of the contract. Behavioral Contracts establish structure and accountability, both of which are scarce in the chaotic life of addiction. Behavior Contracts can be executed between the addict and his sponsor, Bishop, spouse or other trusted advisor or friend.

SAMPLE CONTRACT
Conditions:

I will abstain from my addiction and my drug of choice.
I will attend weekly LDS Family Services Addiction Recovery Groups.
I will report monthly to my Bishop.
I will meet with my therapist twice monthly.
I will read scriptures and pray daily.
I will do something for my recovery every day.

Privileges for meeting these conditions:

After six months of sobriety, we will revisit my moving back home.

Consequences for failing to meet these conditions:

If I fail to keep the contract, we will move forward with legal separation.

Behavior Contracts can be helpful for the addict both in recognizing that a commitment has been made, and that there are consequences waiting upon his behavior.

Putting it on the Altar

Sometimes making change is best practiced in conjunction with ceremony or ritual. Wilderness Therapy counselors might put the name of a problematic behavior, like anger or selfishness, on a rock and add it to a client's backpack. After feeling the added weight that behavior adds to the load of life while backpacking for a week, a ceremony is held in which the client throws the rock off a cliff, symbolically sending away the behavior and lightening his load. The physical events aid in the emotional change, and they emphasize the *I am done with this!* statement.

We also can benefit from this principle by making an event of our giving up our addiction. Consider putting your mind and will on an altar and offering it to the Lord—something like making a sacrifice of your addiction.

Elder Neal A. Maxwell explained the value and goal of the ritual of sacrifice on the altar for each of us. *The real act of personal sacrifice is not now nor ever has been placing an animal on the altar. Instead, it is a willingness to put the animal that is in us upon the altar—then willingly watching it be consumed! Such is the sacrifice unto* [the Lord of] *a broken heart and a contrite spirit* (Maxwell, 1987).

Putting the *animal that is in us* on the altar is the first step; showing that we are willing to watch *it be consumed* by doing the work of recovery is the second. The presence of the Willingness provided by the *broken heart and contrite spirit* gives us the Courage and Commitment to follow through.

Mark put it this was:

> When I first heard about the Third Step, "Decide to turn your will and your life over to the care of God, the Eternal Father and His son Jesus Christ," I got a mental picture of one of the ancient prophets kneeling at an altar of rocks, offering up his devotions. I remembered a favorite spiritual place I had found in the Eagle Cap Wilderness. It had always reminded me of an altar, and, although a difficult trip, I made my way there whenever I could. I always brought my scriptures and engaged in prayer. I can't describe the grandeur of the place the incredible views and majesty all around. I just felt that God was close when I was there.
>
> I thought it was the perfect place to turn my life and will over to Him, so I took a few days off work and went. In that amazing, amazing place, I offered up the sacrifice of my addiction and turned my will and life over to Him. My life has not been the same since.

This is Mark's prayer:

My Father in Heaven,

I am so grateful to you for your presence in my life. The peace and comfort and joy that I feel when you are near are the choicest moments in my life. I am grateful for loving parents who instilled faith in me. I am grateful for your plan for us and the life of your Son. I am grateful for the things you have given me for my care and keeping. I am grateful for a loving wife and wonderful children that have blessed my life. I am grateful for the abilities and gifts you have given me and the opportunities that have come into my life.

Father, I am sorry for my failings. I am especially sorry that I have allowed myself to fall into addiction. I am sorry for the lives that I have hurt and for the emotional things that I have stolen. I am sorry that I have lost myself in my own gratifications and was never concerned about the harms I was causing. I am sorry for the things left undone when I was lost in my addiction and sorry for the acts I committed.

I humbly ask for thy forgiveness for these shortcomings.

Today I am offering my life and my will to thy care and keeping. Please help me find the humility to allow my will to be swallowed up by thy will. Please help me to always put thee first. Help me abandon my selfishness and especially my lust.

Help me build a life based on love and trust, a life that would follow the Savior's example, helping where I can, while always following the commandments. Help me seek opportunity to serve. Help me always have compassion and understanding. Help me leave judgment in your hands. Please allow me to help others find healing.

I thank you for the things I have learned. Even in the struggle of addiction, I have found my faith and learned compassion and humility. For all that has come to me, I am truly grateful.

> *Please bless me in this commitment—that it will ever*
> *be before me, that it will always be in my remembrance,*
> *that it will be my guide, that I will ever be true to it—II*
> *humbly pray in Jesus name, Amen.*

Your Sobriety Survival Plan

This is your Sobriety Survival Plan. It is your bailout plan when you feel like you are approaching the falls. It is how you eject from the plane that undoubtedly will crash and burn. It is your last line of defense, your move of last resort to save your sobriety. It is the emergency exit strategy for when your addiction comes calling for you.

For John, it was the temple grounds.

> *When I felt like I was losing my battle with my addic-*
> *tion and nothing seem to change its relentless pursuit of*
> *me, I would go sit on the grounds of the temple. Sometimes*
> *I would sit in the atrium and just pray or read my scrip-*
> *tures. I was safe there, and I would leave only when I felt*
> *strong enough.*

For others it might be a priesthood blessing. Blessings have very profound, life-changing power.

For one addict, it was driving over to his mother's house to visit her. She was never aware of what he was doing, but he knew he wouldn't act out there. Find a sanctuary of last resort, and hold that option always at the ready.

The Woman with Issue

The Biblical story of a certain woman, who had an issue of blood twelve years, can give addicts insight into the requirements of healing. Her struggle sounds very similar to the progressive disease of addiction. She had *suffered many things of many physicians, and had spent all that she had, and nothing bettered, but rather grew worse.* When she heard of Jesus, she traveled to where he was and fought through *the press* to touch His garment. She said: *If I may touch but His clothes, I shall be whole*: and we know that she did touch the hem of His robe and was made whole.

Like this woman, addicts have long suffered. They have tried many solutions and have expended great effort, but are unable to find relief. Things grow worse, because it is a progressive disease. They might follow this woman's example. Find where the Savior is and travel there, no matter how far or difficult the journey. Under the rules of the Law of Moses, this woman's life and movements were greatly restricted. In spite of her challenges, she was willing to do whatever it took to find Him. And when she did find Him, she fought through the crowd (or press) to be next to Him. Don't we often find true closeness with the Savior the most difficult part of the journey? Our daily lives present so many spiritual distractions that we must fight through to stand next to Him. Yet, that is the place of healing.

If we can find Him, if we can fight through the press and be close enough to touch His garment, then He may say of us: *Thy faith hath made thee whole; go in peace, and be whole of thy plague.*

He is found upstream in the safe, healing Waters of Recovery.

The Benchmarks of Early Recovery

Benchmarks tell us where we are, and when we are being successful. Ron tells this story:

> *My brother and I once took our oldest daughters on a backpacking trip on the Pacific Crest Trail (PCT) in Southern Washington. We were hiking very early in the season and the usual annual trail maintenance work had not yet been completed. We came upon a section of the trail that had recently been processed by a clear cut logging operation. It covered what appeared to be about 160 acres and completely obliterated the trail. The PCT is normally well-marked with frequent, recognizable trail markers that indicate that you*

are still on your intended course. In the devastated area of the clear cut, there were no markers or visible paths to indicate where we should go. We really struggled to find the trail at the edge of the clear cut until we saw our old friends, the trail markers that directed us on our way.

As we move through the recovery process, we can observe trail markers or benchmarks that tell us we are successfully traveling on the path of recovery. They are progressively achieved. They reward our efforts and indicate achievement and progress. They tell the addict that what he is doing is working.

For an addict, attaining the benchmarks builds confidence and faith and raises addiction recovery skills levels. For those around him, his accomplishments in reaching benchmarks indicate that change is taking place in his life.

These benchmarks become monuments of accountability in an addict's recovery. By reaching them, we are testifying in a nonverbal way that we are doing the work, and we are intent on personal change. As our achievement is observed by others, relationships and trust, which have been tested, can begin to be rebuilt.

The Benchmarks for Early Recovery are:

#1. Establishing Sobriety

It is pretty simple. You say you don't want to be an addict any more? Stop using your drug of choice and acting out. Many clinicians are unwilling to take clients into treatment relationships unless they have achieved sobriety. They recognize that healing isn't an option as long as the client is in the grips of regular use. Not achieving sobriety is a roadblock to further recovery. We can't go forward. We can't jump ahead to work on recovery skills, hoping they will help us find sobriety at a future date. It just doesn't work that way. Our work is progressive and sequential and we cannot deviate from that. Sobriety must come first.

#2. Finding Hope

Finding hope is part of the equation that creates the Willingness Attitude of Recovery. When enough faith and desire come together, hope is generated. The absence of hope allows despair to flourish. This despair arrives in the addict after an uncountable number of failed attempts to change and to quit using. The hopelessness is energized and empowered by the addict's shame.

President Uchtdorf states: *The adversary uses despair to bind hearts and minds in suffocating darkness. Despair drains from us all that is vibrant and joyful and leaves behind the empty remnants of what life was meant to be. Despair kills ambition, advances sickness, pollutes the soul, and deadens the heart. Despair can seem like a staircase that leads only and forever downward* (Uchtdorf, 2008). Nobody knows the downward staircase of despair like an addict. He has lost *ambition*, carries a *deadened heart* and lives a life with only *empty remnants*. Before recovery, his only defense has been to use and act out.

The coming of hope is a rather joyous sunrise for the addict. Leaving the dark, heaviness of despair is exhilarating. Feelings return that have been long absent, shame subsides, self-hatred wanes and the thought emerges, *Maybe I can do this. Maybe, just maybe, there is reason for hope.*

#3. Willingness to Do the Work

When we achieve an ability to do the work, we know we have achieved the Recovery Attitude of Willingness. We have gathered enough faith and humility that hope has been generated and a willing heart has emerged.

When Monte J. Brough was called to be a General Authority, he stated: *One thing I have is a willing heart. I am willing to do anything and everything that I can to help this great cause* (Brough, 1988). This is the type of willingness we have to have to be successful at the work of recovery. *Anything and everything that I can* gives us the ability to face down fear, discouragement, our urge to use and our love for our addiction. Anything less leaves us vulnerable.

In his teachings about Church service, Marvin J. Ashton said: *A willing heart describes one who desires to please the Lord and serve His cause first. He serves the Lord on the Lord's terms not his own. There are no restrictions to where or how he will serve* (Ashton, 1988). Our success in recovery would benefit from these same two principles of willingness. We must put our recovery work first, and we can put no restrictions on what we will or will not do to recover.

Addicts who put restrictions on recovery remain addicts. *I don't think those meetings will help me,* failed recovery candidate #1 explained.

Working the steps seems like a lot of busy work, and not very productive, said failed candidate #2.

My work situation is too demanding for me to do all these things you are asking, said failed candidate #3.

If my spouse would get off my back, I could focus on this better, claimed failed candidate #4.

Do you see the pattern here? When we do not put recovery first, or when we put restrictions on what we will or can do to recover, it is the expression of an unwilling heart. An unwilling heart presents the behaviors of resistance and contention. It is a manifestation that dooms our recovery. If we notice resistance and contention among our behaviors, we are in trouble. The remedy is to go back and redevelop the Recovery Attitude of Willingness.

#4. Overcoming the Wall

Addicts often go on a confusing honeymoon with their recovery. The despair of addiction has been their lot. *Why can't I stop? What is wrong with me?* Shame and self-loathing cycles are common and feel like a tremendous weight, pressing down the addict. When change begins, the weight is lifted; the addict's mood changes. Establishing some sobriety, killing secrets by confession and feeling more hope than he can ever remember is heady stuff. It feels good, often euphoric.

That euphoric feeling leads to a mistaken belief of inevitable success. Sex addicts are especially susceptible to this. There is tremendous relief when they have finally made confession and been freed from the burden of their dark secrets. A feeling of invincibility and confidence ensues. Maintaining sobriety is not a challenge. This is the honeymoon period of recovery. It often lasts 45 to 90 days and can be so complete that the addict often wonders: *What is the big problem with addiction? Did I really have a problem?*

As time passes and the honeymoon ends, the addict inexplicably slips back into old acting out behaviors. He is stunned by the addiction's return. As when a campfire roars back to life after we thought it was out, the addict is caught off guard by the return of old behaviors. The experience devastates some. Old shame and despair return and eradicate the budding, newly established hope. The addict then faces the reality of what it means to be addicted.

The *Matrix Treatment System*, developed at UCLA as a treatment option for meth addiction, calls this phenomenon *The Wall*. It is the end of the honeymoon and is the demarcation point of the beginning of real recovery. Naivety about recovery is now gone. The true nature of the enemy is understood. We lost this round to the addiction, and now the real fight is on.

For those who stagnate at this point or feel derailed, return to the beginning and reestablish the Attitudes of Recovery and begin anew.

#5. Making the Move from Discovery to Recovery

There are several things that mark our passage from the Discovery to Recovery Phase of this healing process. Surviving the wall indicates we have truly come to understand our plight as an addict. If we have found godly sorrow and been able to establish and maintain sobriety, we have qualified ourselves for the Recovery Phase.

#6. The Arrival of Serenity

Please recall *The Big Book*'s promise: *If we are painstaking about this phase of our development, we will be amazed before we are half way through. We are going to know a new freedom and happiness...We will comprehend the word serenity and we will know peace.* The arrival of serenity is a very important benchmark. It validates our efforts. It gives new confidence, strengthens our faith and resolve, and brings us a new level of hope and comfort. We are on the right path. We can do this.

Serenity is the state in which spiritually, we feel the presence of the Spirit of the Lord in our lives. We will have drawn closer to Him. Emotionally, we have silenced our emotional storms, we are at peace. Mentally we are aware of a new clarity and a quiet confidence growing within us.

Our ultimate goal is *the mighty change of heart* that comes from the Savior's healing touch. *We seek not just a change of actions, but a change of heart* (Benson, 1989). As we move through the recovery process, we move closer to Him. His Spirit and influence returns to our lives and becomes more recognizable. We begin to listen. We find the ability to respond to the Spirit and its promptings. There is a reason the Holy Ghost is called the Comforter. He speaks the language of peace. He is the originator of serenity.

One of the benefits of serenity is that our recovery work will become even more productive. We are now working from a platform of peace and not from the chaotic, thinking-error riddled world of the addict. We are moving away from Satan's influence. We have new, rediscovered spiritual allies in the Savior and the Spirit. We have taken off the brakes and progress can quicken.

Others will notice a change in behavior and demeanor. We will be present and emotionally available for others at home and at work. Contention will be gone, and we will present a calmness that makes others feel safe in our presence.

With this benchmark, we will be able to note that we have come a long way. It is worthy of celebrating, but it is not the end. There is much more to do.

#7. The Regular Happening of Aha Moments

Aha moments tell us we are getting it. They are moments of clarity and new vision. They are the raw materials from which we build our bridge to recovery. Aha events are moments of new understanding, when we see things in a new light. They indicate that growth and change are occurring.

That which is of God is light; and he that receiveth light, and continueth in God, receiveth more light; and that light groweth brighter and brighter until the perfect day (D&C 50:24).

Aha moments are the act of receiving *more light*. These moments are built upon one another. We cannot have the next experience until we have internalized and had the benefit of time with the previous moment. Martial artists progress through a series of belts, indicating their level of skills. Each new level is taught based on the skill learned at the previous level. Each level prepares for the next. We cannot learn the next skill level until we have mastered our current one. So it is with emotional and spiritual development. We need time and experience to master new skills and understandings before the next opens to our view.

It is not unlike points of interest on a scenic highway. We cannot see them until we have traveled the appropriate distance on our journey. In recovery, we travel by doing our work. Our recovery labor moves us from understanding to understanding as we experience healing.

In gospel language, we would say *line upon line, precept upon precept. For behold, thus saith the Lord God: I will give unto the children of men line upon line, precept upon precept, here a little and there a little; and blessed are those who hearken unto my precepts, and lend an ear unto my counsel, for they shall learn wisdom; for unto him that receiveth I will give more; and from them that shall say, We have enough, from them shall be taken away even that which they have. (Isaiah 28:13)*

As we display willingness (*lend an ear unto my counsel*), we move closer to Him (*here a little, there a little*) and *learn wisdom*. We move toward His healing power in this incremental fashion. As we *learn wisdom*, we feel the desire to change our addictive behaviors or we lose interest in them. It makes less and less sense for us to try to meet our needs with dysfunction.

One way to say to Him that we have enough, is to become involved in addiction. When we seek out comfort from our drug of choice instead of hearkening unto His precepts, we are in danger of losing our testimony and relationship with Him. *It shall be taken away...even that which they have.* We pay quite a price.

Many of us, in our addictions, have experienced that. We have removed ourselves to a place far from Him. Through denial, thinking errors and our addictive practices, we have hardened ourselves and moved away from spiritual things and into Satan's world. *Aha* moments mark our path back to the Savior.

A Word About Time

There is a time factor involved in recovery and healing and we cannot hurry the process. A choir director once explained the process of learning a song for her choir: *After everyone learns the words and notes, there is a settling in period of three or four weeks before everyone really knows the piece.*

Even though the choir members have an understanding of the words and notes, a new piece doesn't become readily available for them to perform immediately. Likewise in recovery, we need time for the things we are learning to settle in and truly become part of us.

Laura Davis spoke of recovery from sexual abuse, but her words also feel crafted for addicts seeking recovery:

> *Over the years I've come to realize that healing is, in fact a process that takes a lifetime. As survivors [and addicts], we need to settle in for the long haul. It's a process that continues for the rest of our lives. Healing is not about quick pain relief. It's about the little steps. It's about learning to take care of ourselves. It encompasses both progress and backsliding. Healing is slow. It's gradual. It does not proceed in a straight line. Healing takes time* (Davis, 1990).

President Benson taught: *We must be careful...that we do not become discouraged and lose hope. Becoming Christlike is a lifetime pursuit and very often involves growth and change that is slow, almost imperceptible. The scriptures record remarkable accounts of men whose lives changed dramatically, in an instant, as it were: Alma the Younger, Paul on the road to Damascus, Enos praying far into the night, King Lamoni. Such astonishing examples of the power to change even those steeped in sin give confidence that the Atonement can reach even those deepest in despair.*

But we must be cautious as we discuss these remarkable examples. Though they are real and powerful, they are the exception more than the rule. For every Paul, for every Enos, and for every King Lamoni, there are hundreds and thousands of people who find the process of repentance much more subtle, much more imperceptible. Day by day they move closer to the Lord, little realizing they are building a godlike life. They live quiet lives of goodness, service, and commitment (Benson, 1989).

Progress in recovery may at times be very dramatic and at times unnoticeable. Things like gaining sobriety produces changes that are visible to everyone. The farther we move upstream from our acting out, the less dramatic the effects of our changes become. Things slow down. The change resulting from the behaviors of advanced recovery takes on this subtle, much more imperceptible characteristic. We may fall into the *little realizing* category. We may even feel done. Our progress in recovery from addiction is just the beginning of building our own Christlike life. It should be our lifetime pursuit. We need to invoke the Attitude of Commitment and *hoe to the end of our row*, no matter how long it takes.

After extended sobriety and recovery, if we begin to feel frustration that things are not changing fast enough, there is still danger for us in *discouragement, which leads to a loss of faith and hope and patience. To those who are discouraged, there is the feeling that "there is nothing I can do to change myself or my circumstances." We begin to accept ourselves as we are, declaring, "That's just the way I am"* (Condie, 1993).

If we learn anything from recovery, it is the incredible human ability for change when we involve Christ in the process. Obviously it is not an easy task. It can be explained briefly in a few pages, but the doing of it is often the greatest challenge of our lives. Patience and long suffering, sometimes required by time, are often spiritual gifts we *earn* or, perhaps better said, receive, in the process of our recovery.

CHAPTER 3

Avoiding the Pull of the Waterfalls

I know there are times when I do not follow the will of the Father for me;
Sometimes I am lazy. I must be more diligent.
Sometimes I am unaware. I must learn His ways.
Sometimes I am defiant. I must humble myself.
Sometimes I am selfish. I must serve Him.
Sometimes I am afraid. I must trust Him.
Sometimes I don't hear Him. I must be more in tune.
(Anonymous from a Recovery Journal)

Walking Down another Street

At this point in the process, our purpose has now become making the
change from the Recovery Phase into the Maintenance Phase of addiction recovery. This is where our tactics need to change. The battle
fronts have moved significantly, and our approach needs to reflect those
changes. In the Discovery Phase, we were fighting to establish sobriety
and learning the awful reality of what being an addict means. We were
beginning to feel some godly sorrow. In this phase, it felt like hand-
to-hand combat every day. By developing the Attitudes of Recovery,
following the Rules of Early Recovery and putting a few tools in our Recovery Toolbox, we found and could maintain sobriety and began healing as we moved through the Recovery Phase. We now find ourselves

far upstream, away from the falls in the safe Waters of Recovery. However, staying there isn't a given. Our task now becomes to maintain what we have gained and continue to grow.

James E. Talmage, in his *Parable of the Defective Battery*, presents the story of his experimental work that relied on a series of batteries for power. One of the 12 batteries was failing. He states:

At the first opportunity of convenience, I gave closer attention to the rejected unit. There was little difficulty in determining the true cause of the trouble. The cell ... had short-circuited itself. Through its unnatural intensity of action, as a result of its foaming and fuming, the acid had destroyed the insulation of some parts; and the current that should have been sent forth for service was wholly used up in destructive corrosion with the jar. The cell had violated the law of right action—it had corrupted itself. In its defective state, it was not only worthless as a working unit, and an unproductive member in the community of cells, but worse than worthless in that it interposed an effective resistance in the operation of the other clean and serviceable units.

That sounds like addiction. Addicts violate the *law of right action* and *corrupt* themselves. Corruption comes by misapplying our emotional system to the struggle of life. Whether we are medicating pain, have developed a shame-based system, were blessed with predisposition or have taken any other path to addiction, thinking errors, denial and the addictive process have corrupted our emotional system. The damage is not confined to just the addict. The addict's family is also devastated; *the effective resistance in operation* caused by the chaos and dysfunction of the addict brings turmoil and hurt into the family relationships.

Talmage continues: *I searched the innermost parts, and with knife and file and rasp removed the corroded incrustment. I baptized it in a cleansing bath, then set it up again and tried it out in practical employ. Gradually it developed energy until it came to work well. Yet to this day I watch that unit with special care; I do not trust it as fully as I trusted before it had befouled itself.* (Zodell, 1973.)

I watch that unit with special care is a statement of Maintenance. Our purpose is maintaining what we have gained and avoiding the slipping back into old ways. We also must learn skills that allow us to watch *with special care* to protect ourselves from the return of our addictive behaviors. Remember Carnes' warning: *Once this point is reached* [addiction], *addicts cannot undo all the damage even with help. Significant shifts have occurred which leave them forever vulnerable to their addiction. Compulsive use always remains an option.* (Carnes, 1992) We cannot walk away from addiction and pretend it never happened. We must defend against its return every day. We must practice Maintenance.

Portia Nelson presents a very helpful way to look at the problem in her book, *There's a Hole in my Sidewalk: The Romance of Self-discovery*:

Walk Down Another Street

Autobiography in 5 Short Chapters by Portia Nelson
I walk down the street.
There is a deep hole in the sidewalk,
I fall in.
I am lost...I am hopeless.
It isn't my fault.

I walk down the same street,
There is a deep hole in the sidewalk.
I pretend I don't see it.
I fall in again.
I can't believe I am in the same place,
But it isn't my fault.
It still takes a long time to get out.

I walk down the same street,
There is a deep hole in the sidewalk.
I see it is there,
I still fall in it...It is a habit.
My eyes are open,
I know where I am,
It is my fault...I get out immediately.

I walk down the same street.
There is a deep hole in the sidewalk,
I walk around it.

I walk down another street.

Nelson captures the story of recovery in this five-chapter poem. Finding the new street is accomplished through our efforts in the Discovery and Recovery Phases; we then walk that new street in the Maintenance Phase.

The Lord makes a promise of leading us on a new path, if we are willing. *And I will bring the blind by a way that they knew not; I will lead them in paths that they have not known: I will make darkness light before them, and crooked things straight. These things will I do unto them, and not forsake them.* (Isaiah 42:16)

In our addiction, we certainly do not know His way; we are especially blind to it. If we can muster the faith and trust, He will truly lead us to paths that we have not known, even down another street. Keeping ourselves in that new path or on that different street is the embodiment of what the Maintenance Phase is about.

Learning to Live in New Territory: Defending Serenity

Obtaining serenity and maintaining serenity are two different skill sets. We often feel the arrival of serenity and bask in its comfort for a time; we assume we have overcome our addiction and serenity will last forever, and then notice it slip away. We haven't yet developed the skills of Maintenance.

> *One year James, put in a new lawn. He meticulously prepared; he spared no expense or effort to install the new lawn. He carefully watered and protected it in those first few months. It was award worthy.*
>
> *In midsummer, he was called away on an emergency business trip that was to last into the fall. He left the care*

of his prize lawn to his teenage son. The son was not quite as invested in the lawn as James, and did not pay it much attention. He mowed occasionally, but did not seem to notice the thistle and dandelion invasion, nor did he pay attention to the arrival of the gophers and moles. The lawn provided dad with a very disappointing homecoming.

James installed a heck of a lawn, but the maintenance program betrayed his efforts. For the addict, gaining sobriety without the skill to maintain it can be just as fruitless.

Ron talks about his experience:

> *When I first felt serenity in my life, I didn't like it much when it left. I wanted the peace and comfort of it to be there all the time. My sponsor told me to think of serenity as a plateau, a plateau that had a steep drop off where serenity ended. My job, once I recognized that I was in serenity, was to defend it. Fight anything and everything that could destroy or end the serenity. I needed to challenge and eliminate from my life, every thought, behavior, action, and emotion that would diminish my serenity. It really helped to think of it that way. I was trying to extend the plateau, to make it as large as I could. My job was to maintain it.*

The maintenance of it is now the key. The *Bible Dictionary* reminds us that *through the grace of Christ we can maintain a good work* (LDS Bible Dictionary, 1989).

Just as our recovery required that we be centered on Christ, so it is with maintenance.

Alma asks: *Have ye spiritually been born of God? Have ye received his image in your countenances? Have ye experienced this mighty change in you hearts?* Then he asks the most important question: *If ye have experienced a change of heart, and if ye have felt to sing the song of redeeming love, I would ask, can ye feel so now?* (Alma 5:14, 26)

If we can still feel *to sing the song of redeeming love,* we have defended serenity. If we continue to experience the *change of heart,* we have mastered Maintenance.

Establish Mooring Lines

Just as ships secure themselves at the docks with mooring lines, we should secure ourselves in the Waters of Recovery with suitable mooring lines.

In these living Waters of Recovery, we find that every thought, behavior, activity, and involvement is free of any element of the addiction. We can think and participate freely and safely, as, here, our thoughts and actions will not contribute in any way to relapse; instead, they are the very elements of recovery and healing.

Here we can establish safety lines that preserve our Maintenance, hold us in place or keep us grounded in recovery. Things like self-help meetings, accountability, sponsors, therapists, Church service and attendance, treatment, scripture study, prayer, meditation, being present to our feelings, self-care, adequate sleep and positive social support, all could be mooring lines that protect us from crossing the line and entering the waters where we feel the pull of the falls.

Finding the Line: In my Addiction/Out of my Addiction

When we are truly in the Waters of Recovery, we are *out of our addiction.* This is a safe place. We are free from the pull of the falls. However, when our thoughts and behaviors cross that dividing line into flowing water, we find ourselves *in our addiction* and susceptible to the building power of the waterfalls. Our addictive behaviors always remain an option, and we can slip back so easily.

There is a significant difference between serenity—the peace we feel in the Waters of Recovery—and the chaos of addictive thoughts and behaviors that are found in the river moving towards the waterfall. Knowledge of this line of separation is a mandatory point of mindfulness for this Maintenance Phase.

An addict must foster and keep a conscious awareness of where the dividing point is and must constantly monitor his thoughts and behaviors in relation to that dividing point. He must always ask himself if he is in or out of his addiction. He must always ask himself if he is in or out of his addiction. In this way, an addict can maintain his position in the safe upstream waters. Inattention to our thoughts, emotions, and behaviors allow us to drift, unaware, into dangerous downstream waters and the return to acting out.

> *Jim was really doing a remarkable job with his recovery. He was a porn addict and a very successful banker with a great deal of responsibility. He threw himself into recovery work like he did everything else, full speed ahead with an all-in mentality. Months went by and Jim was feeling great results in his life from achieving sobriety and gaining some recovery. He had achieved the calmness of serenity. He had the ability to be aware when that peace left him.*
>
> *Then, while he was on a long road trip, Jim had the experience of having his mind wander back to some old pornographic images. The boredom of the drive left him susceptible. He felt his lustful neurotransmitters firing off in his brain and the surge of his addictive pattern returning. He realized he was again in his addiction. He struggled to clear the images and cross the line back to his serenity and safe waters.*

Jim was really in touch with himself and his thoughts and feelings. He has learned the skill of mindfulness, and he knew when he slipped into his addiction. He had established conscious awareness of his emotions and feelings. He recognized that his sobriety could be compromised if he allowed the situation to continue or if he gave place to those old recollections in his mind. He also knew how to get out of his addiction. By clearing the thoughts, his sobriety survived another day, and Jim remained in the Waters of Recovery, rather than being caught in the waterfalls.

When we are in our addiction and have crossed that safe line in the river, we find thoughts, behaviors, activities and involvement that lead to acting out. Like the river's water that picks up speed and power as it approaches the head of the falls, our behaviors in these waters grow in intensity as we move towards acting out.

Many of those thoughts, behaviors, activities and involvements, which are just beyond the point of safety, may not seem dangerous at all. Giving place to reminiscing about the old days, skipping a self-help meeting or missing prayers, may seem harmless, even justifiable, but these are all things on a downstream heading. They are on the wrong side of the line. They are in our addiction, and they put us in proximity of the next level of slippage, toward acting out.

If we take that first seemingly harmless step, the problem compounds. After missing a meeting, we might feel embarrassed to call our sponsor, or after meeting with an old drinking buddy to hang out, we might agree to meet next time at the old watering hole (not to drink, we justify, but to meet up with all the old friends). When we go to the old watering hole, we are inviting relapse, and history tells us our recovery cannot survive in such a setting.

Again, our initial behaviors that cross the line might seem so innocent, justifiable, and non-threatening. However, those innocent and justifiable things, are what take us across the line where we are again in our addiction. We know, then, that the current leads us to the inevitable waterfall.

The pattern is endlessly repeated by addicts. We start with a small misstep and, because we feel we haven't done anything wrong, we keep aimlessly floating downstream. However, the next thing we know we haven't been to a meeting in weeks, and recovery work just doesn't hold our interest, because the lure of the old life is calling us. Without knowing why or how, we are walking out of the store with a six-pack, calling our supplier or searching our favorite porn site.

In the Biblical story of David and Bathsheba, it all began when the king could not sleep and wandered out onto his roof. At this point, the murder of Uriah was not even a remote possibility. *From the roof he saw a woman washing herself; and the woman was very beautiful to look upon*

(2 Samuel 11:2). This was the safe line in the river for David. If he had looked away from that scene, and returned to his bed, his life would have taken a very different course.

Instead, he chose to watch and ponder the possibilities. He crossed the safe line. If we were discussing a sexual addict, he was now in his addiction.

He then *enquired* after the woman. When David learned that this was the wife of Uriah the Hittite, he had another opportunity to leave it alone. Like the addict caught in the strengthening currents of the waterfall, he continued downstream by sending messengers for her. Again, he might have avoided great tragedy, had a pleasant dinner with her and sent her home, but he continued to flow with the ever-increasing current *and he lay with her* (2 Samuel 11: 4).

David went from innocently coming upon a scene, to a curious inquiry, to questionably sending messengers and ending with committing adultery. Each step he took was more inappropriate than the previous step. Each step led to the possibility of greater harm in the next step.

David's demise was one of the saddest in the Old Testament, but his story can help us avoid our own personal tragedy if we learn from him. It is so important to remember that we have no point of greater power than at the line in the river that marks where we move from being in our addiction to out of our addiction. When David stood on his rooftop and choose not to look away, he crossed the safe line. He began losing power and was carried away by the strong currents in the river of lust.

Knowing where that safe line is and knowing the behaviors, thoughts and activities that lie on either side of it is the key to Maintenance. The line becomes our area of battle, our line of defense. We cannot allow ourselves to cross the line and, if we do, we must get ourselves back to safety immediately.

A very helpful exercise in gaining understanding of just where the line is for each us is to conduct a little personal research. Consider, "What is the genealogy of my acting out?" Reflecting on a time when you were acting out, follow the events back to the point where serenity was left behind and you moved into your addiction. Try to find the moment or event that sparked the change. Once the precipitating moment is found, explore what you might have done differently. Keep asking the question: *What else can I do to keep myself safe?*

Become consciously aware of what serenity feels like. We spend so much time on auto pilot that we lose conscious contact with what we are experiencing. When you feel a moment of peace away from your addiction, explore it. Meditate with it. Experience it. Learn it. Know it. Then figure out how to build a monitoring device into yourself that will warn you whenever serenity is disturbed. Whenever your peace is threatened, an internal alarm should go off warning you to get back into serenity.

Clayton learned this way:

> *When I started figuring this out, I decided to say the Lord's Prayer whenever I felt myself crossing the line into my addiction. At first I had to say the whole thing, and there were even a couple of times when I had to say it more than once, but eventually it all became automatic. When my alarm goes off, I realize I have crossed the line, and I say a line or two of the Lord's Prayer. After this, I am back to serenity. It keeps me safe.*

Clayton has found a technique that helps him jump back out of his addiction to serenity. Attending a self-help meeting, singing a hymn, talking with a sponsor or friend, or saying the serenity prayer can also be effective jump-back behaviors.

Developing the mindfulness or mental and emotional awareness, to truly comprehend whether we are in or out, allows us to practice the Attitude of Accountability. The kind of accountability that leads to healing. The kind of accountability that leaves no room for denial, thinking errors or flirting with the edge of our addiction. If we are out of our addiction, we should be able to:

- Maintain the Four Recovery Attitudes: Willingness, Commitment, Courage and Accountability.
- Eliminate contention in all relationships.

- Feel the presence of the Holy Ghost.
- Achieve recovery benchmarks on an appropriate timeline.
- Observe the Rules of Recovery.
- Experience regular, ongoing *aha* moments.
- Use the Tools of Recovery on a daily basis.
- Sustain sobriety and begin achieving recovery.
- Start understanding serenity.

When we cross the safe line in the river to be in our addiction, a change in thinking and behavior sets in. At first the change is imperceptible to the outsider and without the skill of mindfulness, also to the addict. This is the area of the "almost true." It is the spawning ground of thinking errors and denial. Our statements and thinking contain enough truth or justification that they feel correct. Nothing is a blatantly wrong; it is just a little over the line. That "almost true" feel lulls us into thinking we are still safe.

It is not unlike the old tale of cookin' frogs:

Frogs thrown in hot water jump back out immediately and hop away, because they sense the danger. But frogs thrown in room temperature water think it's a great chance for a swim. Even when the heat is turned up, the frogs are relaxed by the soothing of warm water, and they are not alarmed that their safety is at risk. They enjoy the hot tub experience while they are unaware of the ever-rising temperatures. Not recognizing the severity of their predicament, they luxuriate in the moment. They embrace their lot and good fortune only noticing much too late that they are cooked.

Cookin' frogs illustrates an addict's struggle at the edge of his addiction. When we are right at that line between in and out, slipping into the addiction can seem comforting, not dangerous. Our addiction is an old friend that we have been comfortable with for some time. There is enough truth in "almost true" that it feels okay. When we put away vigilance, mindfulness and accountability, getting cooked is not far off.

In 1979, a large passenger jet with 257 people on board left New Zealand for a sightseeing flight to Antarctica and back. Unknown to the pilots, however, someone had modified the flight coordinates by a mere two degrees. This error placed the aircraft 28 miles to the east of where the pilots assumed they were. As they approached Antarctica, the pilots descended to a lower altitude to give the passengers a better look at the landscape. Although both of them were experienced pilots, neither had made this particular flight before, and they had no way of knowing that the incorrect coordinates had placed them directly in the path of Mount Erebus, and active volcano that rises from the frozen landscape to a height of more than 12,000 feet.

As the pilots flew onward, the white of the snow and ice covering the volcano blended with the white of the clouds above, making it appear as though they were flying over flat ground. By the time the instruments sounded the warning that the ground was rising fast toward them, it was too late. The airplane crashed into the side of the volcano, killing everyone on board.

It was a terrible tragedy brought on by a minor error—a matter of only a few degrees (Uchtdorf, 2008).

Gauge settings, off just two degrees, resulted in being 28 miles off course on this very long flight. Our "almost trues" are often only off by just a few degrees. Believing and embracing our almost trues, and leaving the safe waters of recovery, can also take us very far from where we want to be.

Here is a checklist that can help identify the subtle signals that warn us when we have passed from the safety of being out of our addiction to the dangers of being in our addiction:

- There is slippage in maintaining the Recovery Attitudes.
- We might lose our Willingness over such things as being unable to separate ourselves from our user friends or complying with the Early Rules of Recovery.
- Our Commitment might fail us because we become over-confident. We might start thinking that we will never use again, because we have this addiction under control. We might start to struggle to complete recovery assignments such as getting bogged down and not making progress in working the steps. Our attendance at group meetings or Church might become somewhat less than perfect.
- Our Courage may falter and we may fail to stand up for our

recovery and be honest with ourselves. We start blaming others and making excuses, and we begin to feel resentment and become impatient with ourselves and others.

- We let our Accountability slip and lower our standards of honesty. "Almost true" and denial statements and thinking errors begin to surface in our processing.
- We struggle to meet our goals.
- We start thinking we don't need the help of others. We show signs of isolating ourselves.
- *Addict talk* appears. Addict talk is the language and logic we use to allow our addiction to exist. It is the voice of thinking errors, denial, and "almost trues." At the edge of our addiction, we begin to use "set up" logic and language. Here, our language and thoughts begin laying the groundwork for future justification and use. With set up addict talk, we aren't quitting, we aren't refusing, we are just voicing concerns. If we continue to give place to this type of thinking and let it become part of our processing, it will hurtle us downstream to the edge of the waterfall and to acting out.

Some statements we might make as we cross over into our addiction are:

I really miss Jim. Even though he is still using, I think it is all right to hang out with him. He respects what I am trying to do."

Boy, this recovery stuff is easier than I thought. I bet I will be able to drink occasionally.

What a crazy day! I am just too tired to attend my meeting tonight.

I know they want me to get a sponsor, but this is going pretty well and I really don't think I need one.

I don't think I can do this Step 5 work of sharing my inventory with someone else; this stuff is very, very private and really best left in the past.

Man, I am doing all I can do to recover, but there always seems to be something new I need to be doing, and some of it seems like overload to me.

I was trying to get this fourth step done, but my sponsor didn't explain it very well.

I wish they would just cut to the chase and skip all the BS. Some of this recovery stuff doesn't seem very important.

I would like to be able to help with meetings, but there is just no time left in my schedule.

I like going to the meeting, but there is one guy there who really bugs me sometimes I leave when I see his car in the parking lot.

After we have crossed into our addiction, we see incremental increases in addict thinking and behavior. Our violations of serenity become more serious and have greater consequences. We still aren't acting out at this point and may even feel we are a long way from it, but that is how frogs get cooked, isn't it?

"On Our Way to the Falls" Checklist:

Mentally our efforts to be mindful falter, and our awareness of in or out is diminished. Doubts about recovery and the ability to succeed surface. There is trouble staying focused, and the daily routine might be challenging. There is more daydreaming and even the beginning of fantasizing about using.

Emotionally, contention begins to rear its head, emotional storms begin to appear on the horizon, and we may anger easily in our relationships. In addition, worrying may become excessive. Depression, anxiety and fear may take up more of our emotional time. We may desire to isolate away from others and feel like our life is unraveling.

Physically we feel changes: more sickness, new sleep patterns and possibly a general lack of energy. We resort to medications to relieve our discomfort.

Behaviorally our recovery starts to deteriorate. We don't eat well or take care of ourselves. We become more compulsive, often overextending ourselves in trying to please others. We may retreat and practice avoidance. We may struggle to participate in recovery behaviors like group attendance, calling or reading.

Spiritually we lose our conscious contact with the Savior. The spirit feels withdrawn. Prayers are said less often and feel automatic. Spiritual activities such as attending church, teaching, and fulfilling our assignments become chores and we are relieved when we find a good excuse to not participate.

Participating in these thoughts and behaviors, moves us into proximity of the falls and acting out. We have stopped seeking recovery. We still are not ready to act out or use, but we are getting close. The addict is often the last person to notice to the danger he is in. If we continue moving downstream and following the natural progression of our addiction, our ever-deteriorating thoughts and behaviors will take us to the brink:

Mentally we have lost our confidence and spend time worrying about ourselves and our problems. An *I don't care* attitude develops. We may feel a general confusion or feel that our thoughts are out of control. "What's the use" thinking appears, or (its cousin) the idea that using can't make it worse. We may move to suicidal or self-harming thoughts, wondering if everyone wouldn't be better off without us.

Emotionally we become very resentful of others and their behaviors. Anger grows. Deep depression and heavy anxiety appear and may last for extended periods. Emotions are overwhelming, and we begin to feel helpless and hopeless. We may feel extreme loneliness. We feel out of control. Urges to act out appear and are quite strong.

Physically drastic weight gain or loss may take place. We may just feel numb, or we may feel severe lack of energy and cannot get ourselves to exercise.

Behaviorally, we neglect our responsibilities at home and at work. We no longer affiliate with our recovery groups or programs. We are not receptive to those who reach out to us. We experiment with controlled using.

Spiritually, we cut ourselves off from our God. Any involvement in spiritual activities is superficial and makes us feel uncomfortable. Keeping the commandments is not part of our decision-making process (Najavits 2002). The result of continuing this course is that, downstream, we once again pick up our addiction. We have returned to using, acting out and being an addict.

Jump Back Techniques

Jump Back techniques help us move quickly from a position in our addiction to the safety of being out of our addiction. Sometimes we need to make short jumps by singing a hymn, reciting the Serenity Prayer or calling our sponsor. Other situations call for long jumps when we feel far away from the Waters of Recovery. The role of mindfulness and Accountability are to help us hold the awareness we need so that we can know when jumping back is needed. Perfecting mindfulness ensures that our jumps will be short.

Some definitions are helpful to understand at this point:

Slips are very short term returns to our addiction.

Binges are addictive indulges that can be measured in days.

Relapse is the habitual return to our additive behaviors.

Relapse, obviously requires a long Jump Back technique, whereas slips and binges require more modest ones. The thoughts and behaviors that carry us, momentarily, into our addiction can be addressed with short Jump Back skills.

Some things that help addicts Jump Back:

- Go to a recovery meeting.
- Complete an act of service.
- Take preventive action any time you feel Hungry, Angry, Lonely, Tired, or Sick (HALTS).
- Do something nice for yourself.
- Meditate.
- When all else fails, do the work of recovery.
- Ponder on your affirmations.
- Involve yourself in your hobby.
- Get busy.
- Read or write in your Recovery Journal.
- Make something.
- Go to the temple (even if it is just the outside grounds).
- Do some hard exercise.
- See your therapist.

- Practice relaxation techniques.
- Look at yourself in the mirror.
- Walk away from drama or trouble.
- Have a conversation with yourself.
- Connect with others (eliminate any isolation).

Learn enough about yourself to know when you will be vulnerable. There may be places you just cannot go or things you cannot do, because they lead you into your addiction. That is okay. Being safe and sober trumps missing out every time.

HALTS is an acronym preached by AA. Humans are most vulnerable when they are *Hungry, Angry, Lonely, Tired, or Sick.* When any of these manifest, use mindfulness to be aware and find healthy solutions to avoid acting out.

Some become discouraged by addictive thoughts that pop into their minds. Their expectations are often that recovery includes the absence of any thoughts or desires for their addictive behaviors. It does not. Those thoughts will come. They don't mean we are failing at recovery. Remember, we often have spent a long time being addicts. We have become very, very good at it. It takes time to return to thought processing that is free of addiction's influence.

We have little direct control of the thoughts that appear on our mind's stage. They come without solicitation. Our job is to cull through them and discard those that are harmful to us and use only those that are appropriate. We must learn to discard or jump back from those unsolicited thoughts that would return us to the falls.

When Slips Come

Slips, binges and relapses are part of recovery. While many assume these lapses in sobriety mean failure, they, in reality, point the way to success. Recovery is a great struggle—sometimes we overcome it, and other times it overtakes us. Even when we lose, we can learn. Our slips should be treated as teaching and learning moments, not as failures. Slips reveal where the weak points are in our relapse prevention plan. They help us understand what other skills we need and what other changes we ought to make.

One of the characteristics of the early airplanes was their uncertain trip down the runway. They often bounced their way airborne. As they would try to lift off, gravity would pull them down until they found enough speed to create the lift that allows flight. That process of rising up and falling back while still gaining speed describes early recovery. It is very much a process and not an event. We start with very good intentions and experience results that make us think we are ready to fly, and then reality and a slip pulls us back to earth. We learn from our slip, build more speed and try again. Then we slip back to earth again. This process is repeated, until we have mastered the recovery skills that build the speed that creates lift and takes us away from our addiction's power.

Still, experiencing slips and relapse can be devastating. Some cannot tolerate them and, if they slip, they suspend their efforts at recovery. Coach K, basketball coach at Duke University, teaches the concept of *next play*. He wants his players always ready for the next play, unencumbered by the last (regardless if it was a good or bad play). Human nature often encourages us to be concerned about the last play. We are worried about the foul that wasn't called or the missed three-seconds in the key. However, if we fixate on the last play, turn our attention to the referee to plead for fairness, or get lost in our anger, the game goes on without us. Even when we make a great play, there is danger; if we spend time celebrating, the game can also go on without us. When our focus is on the last play, we miss our assignments and hurt our team. There isn't much opportunity in the last play. It is over, the game has moved on. We don't want it to move on without us.

Slips and relapses are like the last play. If we slip, we can get lost in our guilt, disappointment or our failure yet again. Hope takes a hit when we play the recovery game and we are worrying about our last play, our last failure or our lost sobriety. While we fixate on our slip and get lost in our shame, the game and our chance for healing and recovery moves on without us. In our discouragement, we are susceptible repeatedly to acting out. It is a common trap: *I have lost my sobriety, what does it matter now?* At this point, it is easy to divert back to full addiction, and many who experience a relapse do just that.

Although slipping is a normal part of recovery, don't make the mistake of thinking that it isn't a big deal. This is not a free pass for acting out. No one should be flip about losing sobriety. It is certainly not a laughing matter, and no one is saying: *Don't worry about slipping.*

We do not ignore it. We examine it. We learn from it, and repent of it. We move forward with our head in the game ready for the next play.

So, when experiencing a slip or relapse, the following there things are paramount:

1. Reducing the harm (minimizing the damage).

2. Getting back on the horse (returning to sobriety).

3. Examining our slips to build our defenses (relapse prevention) for the future.

Abstinence is our first priority and the ultimate form of harm reduction. If we fail at complete abstinence, then we must fight to minimize the harm and use. Having one drink is better than having a dozen. But, the addict inside of us would have us believe: *Oh well, I smoked a joint yesterday might as well smoke one today.* The reality is we have had a setback,not a capitulation. We are still in recovery, we are not giving up, and we are fighting to contain and minimize the harm.

Returning to abstinence is our second priority. It is important to bounce back after a slip. Picking ourselves up and getting back on the recovery horse puts us back on the path of continued healing. Shame, guilt, disappointment, lack of confidence and our love of our addiction will pull us in the other direction. Healthy doses of Commitment and Courage, two Attitudes of Recovery, can put us back in the saddle.

Learning from our slip is equally important after a relapse. Whenever we move into our addiction and act out, we have made a decision. We need to own that decision and explore our reasoning around it.

Statements like: *Work is stressing me out. I was bored. When my friend asked if I wanted a hit, it just seemed like a good idea* expose thought patterns that commonly accompany relapses. While these statements reveal true needs, they are needs that can be better meet in healthy ways that don't involve using. Finding sober stress reducers, activities that hold our interests or new ways to socialize, meet these needs without involving our drug of choice.

Often, our first excuse or explanation of our slip is not the real one. *Things really piled up on me at work,* is the superficial answer. More accurate would be something like: *I haven't been paying attention to self care, so I can effectively manage my stress.* This points us in the direction of the real solutions. So, look for underlying causes, and don't accept the superficial explanations.

In order to learn as much as we can from slips or relapses, we should ask a lot of questions. They should focus on how the event happened or what can be done to prevent it. Other questions we might ask ourselves:

What was going on that day?

What was I doing? Do I need to avoid this?

Who was I with? Do I need to avoid these people?

Was there a catalytic event? Is this an event I should stay away from?

What feelings and emotions was I experiencing? Are these always problematic for me? What new ways of coping with them can I come up with?

What was I thinking? Did I have stinkin' thinkin or thinking errors?

How did I justify myself at the decision point? How can I dispute this logic in the future?

How did I try to defend my sobriety? How could I have done this more effectively?

Did I reach out to someone? At what point should have I?

In this string of events, what was at the very beginning? When did I cross the safe line, leave the Waters of Recovery, and move into my addiction?

What Recovery Tools did I try to use? What else do I need to do?

How could I have kept myself safe from acting out?

We should take great effort to understand the complete genealogy of our acting out in order to understand and recognize those first steps of addictive behavior. To do this, we should ask ourselves questions: *When did out of my addiction become in my addiction? Where was recovery* compromised? What was the very first thought, behavior or activity that crossed the safe line in the river?

The information we gather can help establish early detection and warning systems. We need to effectively erect watchtowers, as the Nephites did, to become aware of the enemies of recovery at the very first opportunity.

The genealogy for a porn slip might look like this:

- *Boss criticizes addict's work project.*
- *Addict is embarrassed by boss's remarks and shame may be made active.*
- *Addict feels resentment and that the criticism was unfounded.*
- *Anger is given a place to grow.*
- *Addict begins to think he is being victimized at work.*
- *Frustration and feelings of inadequacy monopolize the addict's emotions.*
- *Desire arises to escape these difficult thoughts and feelings.*
- *Addict moves into avoidance and feels relief by staring at a provocative scene.*
- *Addict invites fantasies onto the mind's stage for further self-comfort.*
- *Addict becomes interested in acting out.*
- *Addict finds a discreet computer and logs on.*
- *Addict visits the waterfalls.*

An addict in advanced recovery will recognize the danger he is in when the work is criticized and the hurt feelings arise. He will use new emotional management skills to process the event and stay very far away from any danger of acting out.

By compiling this genealogy, an addict learns that acting out is seldom a random event. He learns that the root of the problem is not only his inability to accept criticism, but also the way his emotional system manages and processes the stressors that result. Finding serenity and healing and getting to the mighty change of heart for this addict has a lot more to do with self-esteem and accepting criticism and the learning of new skills to manage the emotional self, than it does with learning not to turn on the computer.

He does need to find a way to not turn on the computer, but until the underlying issues are addressed and solved, he will be the *dry drunk*. He will continue to experience the dysfunction that led to his using in the past. He will have sobriety, but not recovery. Suffering from the addictive thinking and behaviors will continue and healing will not come.

The genealogy also gives a blueprint for recovery, which often occurs in reverse order of the history:

- *Remove all possible computer access.*
- *Establish mindfulness of where you are in and out of your addiction.*
- *Learn "look away" and other addiction avoidance techniques.*
- *Develop Jump Back techniques when inappropriate thoughts arise.*
- *Follow the Four Agreements. (Don't take things personally.)*
- *Live in the moment and be immune from fears.*
- *Establish healthy levels of self-esteem and be able to accept others as they are.*

We are now ready to explore the Advanced Rules of Recovery. We have found sobriety. Serenity has become our friend. Now we can address advanced skills that will complete our recovery and healing.

The Rules for Advanced Recovery

1. Defend Serenity: Perfect Mindfulness and Conscious Awareness of the Line.
2. Live in the LDS NOW.
3. Pray. No matter how much you are praying it is not enough!
4. Perfect Conscious Contact with God.

5. Develop New Emotional Management Skills: Live in a Drama-Free Zone.

6. Hold NO Expectations.

7. Avoid Cross Addictions.

8. Practice Service.

Defend Serenity

After we achieve serenity, our attention turns to keeping it. We should defend our serenity with all of our abilities and resources, because it is the outward evidence of our healing.

> *William Carney of the 54th Massachusetts was the first black American awarded the Congressional Medal of Honor. He was part of an advance by the 54th on Fort Wagner in Charleston, South Carolina, on July 18, 1863. Some 600 of Carney's comrades started the attack on the fort, which was met with withering fire by the confederates. The sergeant in charge of the company's colors was wounded and fell. Carney threw down his rifle and took up the colors.*
>
> *Carney kept advancing and found himself at the fort's wall, but he was quite alone. The fire had been so devastating that his comrades had either been cut down or turned back. As confederate soldiers moved towards him, Carney returned to federal lines wounded, some four times along the way. The first soldier Carney met on his return trip identified himself as a member of 100th New York and tried to come to Carney's aid by carrying the flag for him. Carney was resistant. He felt he could only turn the colors over to another member of his own 54th. Members of the 54th were hard to find; some 272 of the original 600 men were killed, wounded or missing in action that day.*

*As he returned to his company's line, he was greeted
by cheers, and he finally relinquished the colors to a fellow
member of the 54th.*

We should defend our serenity with the same vigor and courage
that Carney used in carrying the colors for the 54th Massachusetts. It
will sometimes feel like we are under attack. Our addiction's fire may
be withering, we may even feel alone and that our return to using is inevitable. We must find great Courage. By defending our serenity at all
costs, our sobriety can survive.

There are three thoughts that pose threats to derail our sobriety.
Awareness of them, and vigilance against them, will help protect you.
If you find any one of them in your consciousness, dispute it and turn it
over. They are:

I will just have one ...
I can handle this alone ...
I don't care ...

These thoughts are simple and, at times, feel very believable. They are
lies. They relieve us from accountability. We put down our vigilance and
end up liked the cooked frogs, without our sobriety (Najavits 2002).

Perhaps the most dangerous of the three is *I don't care*. It is a product
of frustration, discouragement, and loss of hope. *I don't give a ____, is*
a blank check for our acting out. When we take on that kind of thinking, none of the sobriety skills, goals, commitments or promises matter
anymore. We put away our defenses. We give up. We are especially susceptible when we experience HALTS (hungry, angry, lonely, tired, sick)
or like emotions. To defend our serenity, we must guard against falling
into not caring.

Perfect Mindfulness and Conscious Awareness of the Line

Mindfulness is about two things: Being aware and accepting. Mindfulness is the gateway to living in the moment and bringing the practice
of mindfulness into our lives has a tremendous, lifechanging effect for

good. In our battle with addiction, one of the benefits of mindfulness is gaining conscious awareness of where the line in the river is for us. We must have constant conscious awareness of whether we are in our addiction or out of our addiction.

As we go through our lives filled with stressful events, we often get so used to them and respond so habitually that the play is carried on outside of our awareness. That is, at least, until the weight of our emotional dysfunction will no longer allow that and we break down, physically, emotionally or psychologically. Hence, the need for the awareness of mindfulness.

It is rather a simple idea, but the doing of it, often feels anything but simple. One addict described it this way: *I have come to a personal belief that my spiritual self is very, very mindful, but the physical, human part of me is very, very not.*

That conflict gets in the way, and the practice of being mindful can feel unnatural and foreign to us. Most equate mindfulness with meditation. (The term and practice come from Buddhism and is the seventh element of the Noble Eight-fold Path.) Although meditation can be a very useful tool to teach us how to achieve this state, mindfulness goes far beyond the practice of meditation.

Mindfulness is not being on emotional automatic pilot. Mindfulness is not escaping or avoiding by way of drugs, video games, television or any other means. Mindfulness is awareness of what is going on, both in the world around us and inside of us. Mindfulness also is accepting what is going on in the world around us and inside of us and not creating a reactive emotional firestorm. There is a calmness and peace achieved by mindfulness, because it fosters a sense of comfort and confidence. Mindfulness prepares us to deal with the challenges in our life with all of our emotional energy intact.

One thing that helps us maintain mindfulness is our eternal perspective—that quiet confidence that God is in charge, that He is mindful of us, and that each experience we have is part of our life lesson. We need not fear.

Katelynn was a single mother who had lost custody of her son to the state because a problem with alcohol in her life. She had been able to stop drinking but found the process of working through all the Child Protective Services requirements was very difficult. She was very near to getting her son back but still needed to show that she had appropriate daycare service while she was at work. It was difficult because she started work at a very early hour, and no daycares would accept children early enough to accommodate her. As she struggled to find the services she needed, her anxiety grew. She began to think about what would happen if she could not find daycare. She might have to find a job with better hours, but if she quit her job, she wouldn't have the money for rent and would lose her apartment. She then began to worry about where she would move to and how she could afford it. Her anxiety and fear about her perceived need for a new apartment and job dominated her emotional life.

In the ensuing emotional storms that Katelynn created, she was too distracted to find daycare. The return of her son was in jeopardy. Her immediate need was daycare, but her faulty emotional system fixated on her imagined possible need for a new job and new apartment. The emotional capitol she spent on worrying about her imaginings left nothing for finding daycare. She was exhausted and drained by the self-created anxiety.

Katelynn would have benefited from mindfulness. Remember, mindfulness is about awareness and accepting. Awareness would have helped Katelynn realize she was *future trippin,* worrying about issues that were not yet real. Acceptance would have allowed Katelynn to stay focused on her real issue. Acceptance eliminates the need to worry about our problems in dysfunctional ways. Acceptance allows things to just be.

In colloquial speech, we would say, "It is what it is." Mindfulness is the act of becoming aware of what is going on in the present moment and allowing ourselves to be with what is there—to be able to rest in the awareness of what is there and not be in a frenzy to change it.

That is acceptance. It does not mean we do not look for solutions or that we give ourselves up to our fate. We just don't overreact emotionally to what life presents us.

In Western cultures, we are seldom okay with *what is*. We usually have two solutions to our discomforts of the moment: We either want to attempt to fix it, usually the sooner the better, creating tremendous levels of urgency; or we simply want to avoid it. We want to feel better NOW! We have developed a pill for that solution to every conceived problem. We have achieved a state of believing that suffering is somehow an ancient bedevilment that we have eliminated in our advanced society. We have learned to check out in so many ways. Distractions are available to us at every turn—drugs, alcohol, video games, television, entertainment. We have an amazing array of methods of checking out and avoiding our discomforts.

Consider the alternative Eastern approach, the idea that life *is* suffering. Suffering is not something that needs to be fixed or avoided. Suffering is something we endure as part of our common human lot. Suffering just is. If we can come to accept that philosophy, the management of our emotional lives can change significantly.

The feelings or emotions that we equate with suffering have messages for us. Messages we need to understand and respond to. If we check out, we will miss their direction.

Our emotions were given to us to guide us toward fulfilling our needs. Only when we can be with our feelings and experience them, can we read the message and receive the gift that is in them. Our guilt guides us to better behavior, and our loneliness reminds us we were built to love and be loved.

When we lose contact with those emotions by avoiding in our addiction, or by creating a fixit emotional firestorm, we lose the counsel and guidance of our emotions, the counsel of our true, inner selves.

The role of mindfulness for the addict is to create emotional management that will allow the addict to be in direct conscious contact with his or her emotions. That direct contact allows the addict to monitor where current behavior and thoughts lie in the addiction or out of the addiction. That ability also prepares the addict to live in the moment.

Live in the LDS NOW

The concept of living in the moment or living in the NOW (as described by Eckhart Tolle in his book, *Practicing the Power of NOW*) helps us understand a helpful way of experiencing, managing and living our lives. When we connect those principles with gospel truths, we can achieve a powerful and dynamic way of processing life that unleashes our spiritual selves to thrive.

Unfortunately, we didn't get an owner's manual when we came into this life. Our spirit was not given instructions on how to operate this body that houses it for the sojourn here on earth. We are flying by the seat of our pants and learning as we go. Our parents try to help us, but most of them don't have a clue either about how the spirit and body should interact. We don't know what to do with our feelings and emotions we really don't use our brain's capacity, and we understand little of what our body tries to tell us. We think a lot, but not really very effectively. We struggle through life with a strong desire to do the right thing, but sometimes we feel our greatest enemy is ourselves.

It is rudimentary LDS doctrine that we are spirit children of Heavenly Father and have been placed here on earth in a physical body to gain the experience and lessons of life. The body was provided to help and house our spirits in this process. The body is really a tool of the spirit, a tool that creates our presence and allows the interactions necessary in God's plan for us. If the body is the tool, the spirit is surely meant to be the operator of the tool. The spirit should be in charge of managing, directing and using the tool. Very, very often it is not.

A mindfulness exercise illustrates the point. Clients make themselves comfortable in a position they can maintain for five minutes or so. They are asked to clear their mind of thought and to close their eyes. They are instructed to intently observe the back of their eyelids while trying to keep the mind clear and free from thought. When a thought does appear, they are to take note by saying to themselves, "There is a thought," and let it go. They are instructed to not follow where their thoughts lead them but to return as quickly as they can to their empty mind and wait for the next thought to appear and pass through.

Some notice many thoughts appearing, while others don't; but all are able to observe thoughts coming into their consciousness. The generation of those thoughts is our tool at work, the product of our brain doing its job for us. The observer that notices those thoughts occurring is our spirit. The mind and the spirit—two separate entities. Many misidentify themselves with their mind, often failing to even recognize the spirit's place or existence.

Tolle recognizes the problem when he states: *The greatest obstacle to experiencing the reality of your connectedness* [to your spirit] *is identification with your mind, which causes thought to become compulsive. Not to be able to stop thinking is a dreadful affliction, but we don't realize this because almost everybody is suffering from it, so it is considered normal. This incessant mental noise prevents you from finding that realm of inner stillness that is inseparable from Being* [our spiritual self] (Tolle 1999).

When we fall victim to our own compulsive thoughts, we create emotional storms of anxiety and fear, depression. These storms of emotion disrupt our connection with self. We get lost in them. We lose our ability to be in and experience the present moment. Like violent thunderstorms or tornados, these emotional storms can lay us emotionally desolate. They can leave us unable to manage even the easiest of normal living tasks. We often seek shelter from them in our drug of choice, which further estranges us from ourselves and the life experience found in the moment.

Tolle continues: *The mind is a superb instrument* [tool] *if used rightly. Used wrongly, however, it becomes very destructive. To put it more accurately, it is not so much that you use your mind wrongly—you usually don't use it at all. It uses you. This is the disease. You believe that you are your mind. This is the delusion. The instrument* [tool] *has taken you over.*

So our goal becomes developing conscious contact with our spirit and allowing it to assume its rightful role as operator to manage our lives. That can only happen when we live in the present, in this precise and present moment. Right now. It cannot happen in the future or in the past, where our mind often likes to fixate. When we spend our time thinking about the future or the past, we are creating emotional storms of anxiety, fear or depression. We often place our mind in the past or future to avoid what we perceive as the unpleasantness of the present, and are thereby unavailable to attend to our spirit and our present needs.

Some guidelines for finding the spiritual self:

Our spiritual self can only be located when our mind is quieted and still. (Turn off the brain tool for a moment.) A very effective way of quieting our mind is to intently observe the information that our senses are providing us. What do you see, what do you feel, what do you taste, what do you smell? Observing what we see slowly and intently can bring us the calm and peace that comes with being in the moment. Become aware of the car...the tree...the bird...the house...the child...the bicycle...Victims of panic attacks can find calm in only a few minutes by focusing intently in this way.

With our mind power alone, it is futile to try to grasp or force a connection to our spirit. The spirit lies just beyond our mind's understanding, but it can be felt when we are able to bring ourselves into the present moment.

Place yourself in the position of the observer or operator. Maximize awareness of emotions, thoughts and behaviors. (Maximizing awareness is quite different from fixating and re-numerating, which can create the emotional storms.) Notice them, recognize them, but do not get lost in them.

Observe the feelings of the Spirit derived from your new awareness and connection with Christ. These manifestations of thought and feelings allow us to observe the spirit within.

Pray. No matter how much you are praying it is not enough!

The Savior commanded that we must *watch and pray always lest ye enter into temptation* (3 Nephi 18:18). His command is straightforward. *Watch and pray ALWAYS.* We constantly need to be in contact with our Father—conscious contact. This kind of mindful, conscious contact allows us to be directed on our path. If we turn our mind and will over to Him for His care and keeping (Step 3 of the Twelve Steps), we need constant direction as to His will for us. We only receive that direction as we ask for it.

Alma instructed that when we are not voicing a prayer, our hearts should be feeling one.

When you do not cry unto the Lord, let your hearts be full, drawn out in prayer unto him continually for your welfare and also for the welfare of those who are around you (Alma 34: 27). Again, reiterating that we should continually seek contact with Him, Alma also gave this direction: *Counsel with the Lord in all thy doings, and he will direct thee for good: yea, when thou liest down at night lie down unto the Lord, that he may watch over you in your sleep; and when thou risest in the morning let thy heart be full of thanks unto God; and if ye do these things, ye shall be lifted up at the last day* (Alma 37: 37).

While said in a different way, *counsel with the Lord in all thy doings* refers to constant conscious contact with the Father. Getting counsel and direction is a blessing of its own, but—what addict would not rejoice in receiving the additional promise of being *lifted up at the last day?* After all the struggle and frustration and failures, if we truly seek to ultimately be lifted up, and if we want that blessing, we must make and keep conscious contact with Him.

You can't do it alone ... You need the help of the Lord ... and the marvelous thing is that you have the opportunity to pray, with the expectation that your prayers will be heard and answered...he stands ready to help (Hinckley 1997).

Elder Holland reminds us: *Every time we reach out, however feebly, for Him, we discover He has been anxiously trying to reach us* (Holland 2006).

We probably shouldn't keep Him waiting any longer; no matter how much you are praying, it is not enough.

Perfect Conscious Contact with God

AA's 11th step in the Twelve Step program reads: *Sought through prayer and meditation to improve our conscious contact with God as we understood Him, praying only for knowledge of His will for us and the power to carry that out.* The goal of this step is to gain awareness and to bring into our consciousness an understanding of God's will for us.

Dr. Wayne Dyer explains that in establishing conscious contact: *We can come to know God rather than know about God* (Dyer 2005). Conscious contact can move us from the place of an intellectual belief in God to knowing His love, compassion, mercy, tenderness, forgiveness and power by way of experience. He and His qualities become reality because we have benefited from them, and felt them. When He has wrapped us in His arms and conveyed His never-ending love for us, our relationship is no longer in any way intellectual because *we know Him.*

We need conscious contact because we can't see the big picture. He can. Sometimes we are doing the best we can. We are very busy, sometimes even doing good things, but He has a different good thing in mind. We can be so attentive to our own agenda, so immersed in what we are doing, that we miss His direction to us. We may not be doing bad things, we may not be seeking evil, but if we lose our conscious contact and become inattentive to Him and His promptings, we can still be unaware of His will for us.

President Thomas Monson tells of a personal experience:

That day I felt the unmistakable prompting to park my car and visit Ben and Emily, even though I was on my way to a meeting.

It was a sunny weekday afternoon. I approached the door to their home and knocked. Emily answered. When she recognized me, her bishop, she exclaimed, "All day long I have waited for my phone to ring. It has been silent. I hoped that the postman would deliver a letter. He brought only bills. Bishop, how did you know today is my birthday?"

I answered, "God knows, Emily, for He loves you" (Monson 1991).

Even while on the way to a meeting, busy keeping commitments, President Monson did not lose his conscious contact and when the prompting came to go elsewhere, he heard it and responded. Being able to recognize the unmistakable promptings is *conscious contact.*

All kinds of things get in the way of establishing our relationship with Him, but they all seem to be on our end. He is constant. He is always there. We are the ones who lose the connection. He waits upon us. That thought is depicted in the painting by Warner Sellman, *Christ Knocking on the Door,* presenting the waiting Christ at the door...waiting for us to let Him in. It's quite a conundrum that we run around so frantically seeking peace, happiness and understanding in all the wrong places, while he waits upon us at the door. If only we would just open it.

Early radio was marked by somewhat constant adjusting of the dial to hear the broadcast signal. The broadcast signal to the radio connection was a bit fragile. When the signal disappeared from our radio, it was not because the signal was not there. The broadcast continued, we just lost our ability to hear; it required our attention and adjustment to maintain. Like these old radio connections, our conscious contact is also fragile and calls for constant, attentive adjustment.

Perhaps the greatest blessing conscious contact offers to addicts is its healing power. When we come to *truly know* Him, things change. Our hearts and souls begin to heal. When we experience His love in a very intimate, personal way, our drug of choice just doesn't seem that important anymore. Acting out or anything that moves us away from that healing, connected relationship becomes less important and has less claim on us. As we continue healing, our hearts change, and it truly is a mighty change.

Develop New Emotional Management Skills:
Live in a Drama-Free Zone

The Waters of Recovery are a drama-free zone. No drama queens or kings allowed. Several of the Rules for Advanced Recovery have been about building healthy emotional management skills. Mindfulness, living in the moment, and conscious contact with God are all powerful tools that create healthy emotional systems in us. Many people, especially addicts, fall into an unhealthy management system called the Drama Triangle. The Triangle provides players with a false sense of fulfillment, accomplishment and importance. It is a counterfeit of healthy emotional management. In reality, it fosters shame, helplessness, hopelessness, victimhood, blaming, powerlessness, guilt and manipulation.

A product of the transcendental movement of the 1970s, the Drama Triangle was developed by Steven Karpman. Karpman described an emotional game suitable for one, two or three or more players. There are three roles or positions played in the game, but players often switch roles and exchange positions for the sake of continued play. Karpman described the roles as "Persecutor," "Rescuer" and "Victim," then he arranged them in a triangular fashion:

The Persecutor is an active blamer, who likes to say, "This is all your fault." He can be hypercritical, feels comfortable being angry and often takes a very rigid stance while setting strict limits unnecessarily to create blaming opportunities. The Persecutor's main role in the game is to establish and maintain a victim and to keep the victim feeling oppressed or in victim stance. One of the antidotes for the Drama Triangle is learning to recognize when a victim is being created or played. It is someone taking a victim stance that announces that the game is on. Stopping the game only requires refusal to create or take the victim's stance.

The Victim is personified by the poor-me attitude. The Victim is always looking for the third player, the Rescuer. The Victim doesn't like making decisions. He feels helpless and often hopeless. The Victim is ashamed and, by the descriptive name, feels victimized. The Persecutor and the Victim can both engage in creating a victim, or they can jump in as a Rescuer to continue the game. Yes, the victim can create a victim "in house," with phrases such as "I wish John was nicer to me. I am such an idiot." In saying self-disparaging words, we create the victim. We become our own persecutor, creating the victim's role for ourselves.

Rescuers maintain the "Oh, please let me help you," position. Rescuers feel guilty if they don't help, but their helping fosters dependence in the victim and even conveys the message that it is okay to fail. Rescuers will rescue, even when they don't want to, and they often expect that their attempts will fail, which fosters the "everything really is hopeless" spirit of the game.

Everyone in the game benefits by feeling a sense of purpose and value through the blaming, rescuing and victimization. It is, however, all an illusion, and the dysfunction of it is destructive and keeps us trapped in feelings of shame that the game generates. Addicts especially enjoy the game, because they love their shame, and the fury of blaming and rescuing can create quite a false sense of accomplishment.

To stop the game, don't play. This game does take on a dance-like character as the players respond to another's play or action with a play or action of their own. The Persecutor blames, the Victim is created and takes his stance, and the Rescuer moves in to help. The game can be halted by not responding to the previous play. Don't dance; when the roles aren't played, the game stops.

> Linda was from a well-to-do family of five girls. They were all attractive and outwardly successful women. They played the Drama Triangle game with a vengeance. The game's director was their mother, who constantly used the phone to ask "Have you heard what _____ did? She was offended by someone continually, and particularly focused her scorn and blaming on the family scapegoat, Linda. Linda grew to feel great anxiety over any family event and, especially, phone calls from her mother.
>
> One day, Linda decided she didn't want to play anymore. She wrote a loving letter to family describing how she felt and announcing that she wanted to be part of family activities but that she would not play any part in blaming, victimizing or rescuing. Her letter was met with silence for a few weeks, and then phone calls came one by one. "Yes, you are right, let's not do that any more." Even mom eventually reconciled to the fact that the family might be better served by a different game. Linda was amazed at the game's sudden demise.

Linda's family dysfunction went away when she refused to play, even after it had been played for many years. If we do not react in our role, the game cannot go on, and no one receives the dysfunctional benefits of playing. This is the way to end the Drama Triangle's devastating influence on our emotional lives.

Hold NO Expectations

AA warns us: *Expectations are resentments waiting to happen.* Without doubt, unwarranted expectations are the downfall of many. The House of Israel learned of a coming, promised Messiah. They built the expectation that He would be a very powerful man, who would control armies and nations. When the humble babe was born, and He lived out His life perfectly with nowhere to lay his head, His chosen people could not recognize Him. This carpenter's son from Nazareth did not fit their expectation. He truly was the promised Messiah and fulfilled His role perfectly. That was not the problem. The problem lay in that He did not meet the expectation of a conquering hero. Their expectation blinded them and led them to crucify their very Savior.

Expectations, when unmet, result in all kinds of emotional difficulties.

> *Bob and Sally, who were happily long married, arrived a half hour early to a meeting. Bob was thinking, "Great, I can catch part of the ballgame." Sally thought "Great, we can have a quiet, intimate moment and cuddle." Bob became irritated when Sally was trying to put her arm around him while he was trying to find the game on the radio. Sally got mad when Bob pushed her away so he could fiddle with the stations. The result? Two people who were upset, all because of unmet expectations.*

Some confuse hope with expectation. They are quite different. We get in big trouble when we turn a hope into an expectation.

> *John really worked hard on his recovery and convinced himself that when he reached his one-year anniversary of sobriety, he could relax and enjoy life again. He wouldn't need meetings or the fellowship of others in recovery. "If I don't use for a year, I am not an addict anymore," was his*

expectation. He fell back into his addiction shortly after his one-year anniversary. His expectation betrayed him and caused him to stop doing the things that recovery maintenance requires.

We have every right to hope for healing, but when we turn our hope into an expectation, we generally find disappointment and frustration.

Sadrach, Meshack and Abed-nego demonstrated having hope without holding expectation. When they refused to bow down to his golden image, King Nebuchadnezzer was *full of fury,* promised them a date in the fiery furnace, and asked, *Who is that God that shall deliver you out of my hands?*

The three expressed hope without expectation perfectly when they said: *Our God whom we serve is able to deliver us from the burning fiery furnace, and he will deliver us out of thine hand, O king.*

But if not, be it known unto thee O king, that we will not serve thy gods, nor worship the golden image which thou has set up (Daniel 3:17,18).

Their hope was deliverance from the furnace, and they knew their God could deliver them. They also knew that it was His decision to make not theirs. They held no expectation that their deliverance was something they deserved or were entitled to.

"But if not ..." is a phrase for each addict to understand. We hope for healing from our addiction, and we know it is within the Savior's power. We also know He will give it in His due time. We often, because of expectation, get done before He does. We lack the eternal view. We wonder where our healing is, because we get tired of waiting.

Our attitude ought always be: *"I know the Savior can heal me and deliver me from this addiction, but if not, I will continue to rely on Him, and do all in my power to recover."* That hope, not expectation will carry us home.

Avoid Cross Addictions

One recovering addict puts it this way: *Substance addiction tends not to be confined to a particular mood-altering drug ... when you have on addiction,* you get the whole set thrown in for free—even before you have experienced the other drugs (Bloch 2009). That is cross addiction, and it complicates the recovery of many.

Cross addiction becomes a problem for several reasons. Those predisposed to addiction or those hard wired for it do not cure the predisposition when they stop using. The same forces that brought them to their original drug of choice will be trying to pull them to a new one.

Remember Dr. Carnes warning that when we have become addicted, things have changed neurologically in our brain, and compulsive use is always an option. The brain isn't very particular about what compulsion we use. A new drug will often operate in the brain in a very similar fashion to our original drug of choice.

A third danger is that one of the reasons we got on board the addiction train in the first place was to feel better. The pleasure of the mood-altering substance drew us in. Whether medicating pain, quieting anxiety or depression, or just avoiding boredom, we sought to feel better.

As we went deeper into our addiction, our drug of choice became our ultimate emotional coping skill. When we stop using, we stop having a coping skill. (Even though it was not an effective coping skill, we relied on it to manage our emotional life.)

Fast forward to two months of sobriety: The challenges of life we all face are coming at the recovering addict, but he is not allowed to use his coping skill. That can be problematic. Coping with life can be very, very challenging, and, sometimes, the best answer seems to be find a new drug of choice.

Prescription meds, pain relievers, muscle relaxers, (even the psychotropics for anxiety and depression), over the counter cold meds, the array of illegal drugs, alcohol and some of the process addictions (gambling, sex, and food) are especially inviting to addicts as cross addiction alternatives.

Sally was off methamphetamine but had a prescription for valium because of back pain. She always ran out of pills long before the prescribed period. She justified her use by explaining it was the only way that she could keep working, even though she worked half of the month without any pills because of her misuse of them. She wasn't making much progress in recovery and had increased her drinking ("just a few beers to relax after work," she said). One day, Sally had a run in with Child Protective Services and was threatened with the loss of her children. Looking for alternatives, she changed her pain med to a non-narcotic. With that change and continued Narcotics Anonymous attendance, over time, her need to drink mysteriously disappeared along with other addictive behaviors.

We are still addicts until we stop using in all of its forms.

The threat of cross addiction emphasizes the need to address underlying issues and find new life management skills. Only when we heal from those issues that cripple us and develop new life coping mechanisms, can we move away from the pull of compulsive use.

Practice Service

Whittier wrote the Quaker proverb:

Thee lift me, and I'll lift thee
And we'll both ascend together.

Service is unalterably connected with healing. The practice of service often gets lost with our "me-first" mentality. The Church's Addiction Recovery Program lists Service as the title to its final step. Step 12 involves service to others, *that ensures a continued recovery and a remission of sin. To remain free of addiction, you must get outside yourself and serve. The desire to help others is a natural result of spiritual awakening* (LDS Family Services, 2005). Addiction forces us into secrecy that leads to isolation. We can't be very good at our addiction if we are not isolated. One of the blessings of service is that it destroys isolation.

...The "isolated self" shut off from the Light of Christ makes us become fallible—open to delusion. The balance and perspective which come from caring about others and allowing others to care for us form the essence of life itself. We need the inspired help of others to avoid deceiving ourselves (Hales, 1977).

That alone is argument enough to practice service, but President Monson provides further insight to this act: *The Savior set a powerful unmistakable example of service and commanded us to do likewise. An attitude of love characterized the mission of the Master, He gave sight to the blind, legs to the lame, and life to the dead. Perhaps when we [face] our Maker, we will not be asked, 'How many positions did you hold?' but rather, 'How many people did you help?* (Monson, 2009).

It is impossible for the Savior to personally to do all the good that He would have done. He needs willing partners that also have an attitude of love, people that can get out of themselves and reach out and help others.

Many addicts, as they experience recovery, find in themselves a new empathy and compassion for others. Having been to the brink of self-destruction and back with their addiction, they have gained new understanding for the struggles and trials that others face in life. Compassion and empathy are in short supply in our world of struggle. When we use our new gifts and we extend our love, compassion and empathy to others, we not only help them face another day, but we also find healing within ourselves.

He who lives only unto himself withers and dies, while he who forgets himself in the service of others grows and blossoms in this life and in eternity (Hinckley, 1997).

Service is like the makeup work of our school days. It is has the effect of a do-over. When we come to practice service in the spirit of love for others, that true spirit of charity, we can make up for many things. Peter suggested: *Above all things have fervent charity among yourselves; for charity shall cover the multitude of sins* (1 Peter 4:8).

Moroni's provided a definition of charity when he explained, *If ye have not charity, ye are nothing, for charity never faileth...cleave unto to charity, which is the greatest of all, for all things must fail—But charity is the pure love of Christ, and it endureth forever and whoso is found possessed of it at the last day, it shall be well with him* (Moroni 7:46-47).

Practice service. Learn to love and serve others and it also shall be well with you.

Advanced Recovery Tools

Now some advanced tools for our use as we continue the journey that is recovery.

Don't Underestimate the Light of Christ

Often those that find themselves excommunicated from the church feel very lost and alone. Losing Church membership and the gift of the Holy Ghost can feel devastating. We feel the pain and loss of being cut off. We often view the Holy Ghost as our connection to God. There is a particular aloneness that comes from having that connection severed. We feel very, very far from home with no way of keeping in touch. But we are not left alone.

From the LDS Bible Dictionary, we learn that the light of Christ is *enlightenment, knowledge, and an uplifting, ennobling, persevering influence that comes upon mankind because of Jesus Christ.* It is also the *light that quickeneth* man's understanding (See D&C 88:6-13, 41).

In this manner, the light of Christ is related to man's conscience. It tells him right from wrong and provides insight and inspiration. *The light of Christ will lead the honest soul who "hearkeneth" to the voice.* If we find ourselves without our membership in the Church, finding the voice of the light of Christ is a key tool of recovery.

This is Ron's story:

> *A few months after my excommunication, I visited a couple that I had met through a business transaction. They invited me to dinner out of gratitude for the work I had done. As I approached their door, I felt an old familiar*

feeling. I dismissed it at first. These people were not members of the Church and did not have the Gift of the Holy Ghost, so why would I feel the spirit here? We had a pleasant evening. I learned they were very faithful Christians who took their faith and the practice of their religion very seriously. The feeling of the spirit persisted for me and made me very curious. I made an excuse to drop by a few weeks later to see if I would feel the spirit again. The comforting influence was again present. And each ensuing visit yielded the same results. I pondered on the why of it for some time. I came to understand that these good people had found and magnified the light of Christ in their lives. I realized it is available to all and even I had the ability to access it. From that moment forward I sought it with all my heart, and found in it a great source of comfort, wisdom and encouragement.

Ron's story should give encouragement to all that have lost their Church membership. Seek the light of Christ in your life.

Self-Care

The addict's idea of self-care has little to do taking care of self. It has to do with using–with using things that hurt us. We use with little regard for the long-term damage we are doing to ourselves because we just need to feel better right now. We use way too often and way too much in our self-destructive search for moments when we feel comfort.

The World Health Organization defines self-care as *activities individuals, families, and communities undertake with the intention of enhancing health, preventing disease, limiting illness, and restoring health* (World Health Organization, 1983). For the addict, self-care is about healing first and then about growing. It is about filling our lives with activities and behaviors that nurture self. It means finding and participating in activities that may be fun, but more importantly, create joy and pleasure in healthy ways. Self-care is the process of maintaining the health of body, mind and soul.

The following are some examples of good self-care activities:

- Read a book.
- Take a walk.
- Travel.
- Hang out with safe friends.
- Go to the movies.
- Keep a hobby.
- Express appreciation.
- Love yourself.
- Take a sabbatical.
- Visit the wilderness.
- Donate blood.
- Give unwanted items to Deseret Industries.
- Learn a craft.
- Pull weeds.
- Look at clouds.
- Hold a baby.
- Sit by the fire.
- Sing or whistle a tune.
- Accept a compliment thankfully.
- Waste some time.
- Take in a concert.
- Make a short term goal for self-improvement.
- Play or watch sports.
- Finish a project.
- Write a thank you note.

- Care for a pet.
- Go to bed early.
- Be gracious.
- Join a club or service organization.
- Become a volunteer.
- Laugh at yourself.
- Take a class.
- Let it be about someone else.
- Learn to play an instrument.
- Listen to music.
- Play games,
- Practice meditation.
- Dance.
- Observe the beauty in the world.
- Church attendance and involvement,
- Exercise.
- Bake something.
- Become a volunteer.
- Keep a journal.

For those in recovery, excess and cross addiction are always concerns and always possibilities. Some activities that we view as healthy in moderation may become problematic in excess (Najavits, 2002).

Some examples of self-care activities that may become problems if done in excess include:

- Eating
- Sleeping
- Shopping
- Gambling

- Watching television
- Work
- Exercise
- Internet use
- Video games
- Sex

Compulsivity is an indication that you may be misusing self-care activities (thus, facing potential addiction). When you are compulsive with an activity, use it to alter your mood improperly or employ it to avoid feelings—despite that it harms yourself legally, physically, socially, financially or personally—then that activity has become a problem.

Self-care helps us value ourselves. When we value ourselves, we empower ourselves. When we empower ourselves, we gravitate towards growth and healing and away from dysfunction and addiction.

Four Agreements

Miguel Ruiz, in his work *The Four Agreements*, shares the ancient wisdom of southern Mexico's Toltec. In Toltec, there were scientists and artists who formed a society to explore and conserve the spiritual knowledge and practices of the ancient ones. They came together as masters (naguals) and students at Teotihuacan, the ancient city of pyramids outside Mexico City, known as the place where Man Becomes God. Ruiz, himself a descendent of the Toltec naguals, set forth a way of life, distinguished by the ready accessibility of happiness and love (Ruiz, 1997).

These four wisdoms are a useful, simple guide to keep us in the Waters of Recovery. The wisdoms direct us to behavior and choices that will keep faith with our healing and recovery.

The First Agreement

Be impeccable with your word. Speak with integrity. Say only what you mean. Avoid using the word to speak against yourself or to gossip about others. Use the power of your word in the direction of truth and love.

The Second Agreement

Don't take anything personally. Nothing others do is because of you. What others say and do is a projection of their own reality, their own dream. When you are immune to the opinions and actions of others, you won't be the victim of needless suffering.

The Third Agreement

Don't make assumptions. Find the courage to ask questions and to express what you really want. Communicate with others as clearly as you can to avoid misunderstandings, sadness and drama. With just this one agreement, you can completely transform your life.

The Fourth Agreement

Always do your best. Your best is going to change from moment to moment; it will be different when are healthy as opposed to sick. Under any circumstance, simply do your best, and you will avoid self-judgment, self-abuse and regret (Ruiz, 1997).

The Four Agreements are simple, profound guidelines for life. If we can observe them, we will keep ourselves in safe waters.

Make a Statement of Change

Sometimes addicts have difficulty reconciling the past and moving forward. The weight of their old behaviors can be oppressive and stifling. They carry so much guilt and shame that depression disables them. They feel unworthy and incapable and the future does not feel very inviting to them. At this point a written document, called a Statement of Change, can help move the addict off of top dead center.

A Statement of Change has three elements:

1. A statement of recognition and acceptance of the past.

2. A mission statement.

3. Directions and affirmations.

The following is a sample of a Statement of Change. It was written by Belinda, a 36-year-old single mother recovering from addiction:

> *My life has really taken some detours I didn't plan on. My drugs really messed me up and kept me from being a good mom and a good person. I did a lot of things that I am ashamed of. I have felt, in the past, that I was not good enough.*
>
> *But I am ready to move on now. I am ready for the rest of my life, ready to make changes and leave the past behind me. I want to reclaim my life. I recognize that I am good enough, and more.*
>
> *I am going to stop using drugs. I am going to be more self-reliant and not wait for others to rescue me. I have a lot to offer the world. It is time I started offering. I want to help others, and I am going to finish my college and start working in the healthcare field. I am going to be successful and happy...I deserve that...*

Statements of Change should be recorded in our Recovery Journal and read daily. They serve to remind us of what we are about and keep us on course.

Use Affirmations

Affirmations are positive statements that we can repeat to ourselves to help fight negative thinking and low self-esteem. Affirmations are sound bites that help heal the wounded. Many people are put off initially by the idea of affirmations; it feels silly to some to repeat them. But they work! This is an opportunity to exercise and strengthen our hope and commitment. Repeating affirmations on a regular basis can have very profound results.

- *I am a son/daughter of God; I have a divine spirit and divine potential.*

- *I declare my intention to come to Christ and his healing.*

- *I am willing to experience healing on His terms and schedule, not mine.*

- *I am learning to let go of my need to worry over, or try to control, the things I cannot control.*

- *I have come to understand there are gifts for me to find in my healing.*

- *I invite the help of others in my healing. I seek the supportive blessings of friends and family, past, present, and future.*

- *As I continue to heal, I know that my weak things shall be made strong.*

- *I used my addiction to hide from fear, anger and guilt, but I am learning to face them now.*

- *I know there will be blue days, when I feel sorrow, guilt, shame, anger, frustration and discouragement, but it is part of the healing process.*

- *He has said, "I give unto men weakness that they might be humble; and my grace is sufficient for all that humble themselves before me."*

- *I have learned that through the grace of Christ, we can maintain a good work.*

- *I am developing conscious contact with my inner self and with my God.*

- *I am seeking to come unto Christ.*

- *I am getting better at being kind and gentle with myself.*

- *More and more, I am not accepting my intentions as signs of progress, only my behaviors.*

- *This day, and every day, I need to do something for my recovery.*

- *When I follow the Savior, I know I am on the right path. I can feel His love wrap around me.*

- *I know I don't have to fix it all today. I seek steady progress ... one day at a time.*

- *If there is a high road, I want to be on it.*

- *I am making choices that favor me.*

- *It is becoming more obvious to me, that I deserve my own love, forgiveness, and compassion.*

- *I know the Savior's arms are outstretched towards me.*

- *I affirm my faith in God and His Son Jesus Christ.*

- *I desire that He would say to me as He has said to others, "I see that your faith is sufficient that I should heal you" (3 Nephi 17: 8).*

- *I am gaining a sense of peace and serenity within myself.*

- *I will extend patience and forgiveness to others and myself.*

- *I applaud my ability to survive and my courage to seek healing.*

- *Even when I am overcome with darkness, I know my spirit shines brightly within me.*

- *My spirit and my true inner self can never be diminished or destroyed.*

- *I am coming to understand that my suffering has meaning and that I will come to understand more and more it over time.*

- *I know that I am held in the loving hands of my God...that I am perfectly, utterly safe (Napasstek, 2004).*

Affirmations should be used daily. There are many recorded affirmation products which usually include music. They can be extremely effective in keeping us grounded in our recovery.

Read Your Recovery Journal

In the pages of our Recovery Journal, we find messages that encourage, rejuvenate recovery and teach. We are reminded of how far we have come and the progress we have made. When we reread scriptures and thoughts that had great meaning for us, or experience our life-changing moments again, those healing feelings come back to us.

It can be our own Book of Revelation as we read the revelations that life and the Lord have given us on our journey. We need to be reminded of those healing messages and our purpose. We are strengthened and fortified each time we read them.

These revelations and messages, recorded in our Recovery Journal, can become our own personal scriptures, and we can harvest their power over and over as we reread our entries. We find that new understanding emerges as we revisit these old friends. We develop the capability for greater understanding as we heal and grow, our insight deepens and new things are opened to our view.

20 New Coping Skills

The list that follows includes approaches to coping with life, which can serve as reminders and keep us on track:

1. Remember a setback is not a failure, it is just a setback.
2. Do something to nurture self every day.
3. Move out of your comfort zone.
4. Practice liking yourself.
5. Find your voice, and learn to express what you think and feel.
6. Play out the consequences tape before you act.
7. Trust the recovery process.
8. Bow your head and do the work of recovery.
9. Listen to your needs.
10. Bring structure and organization to your life. Eliminate the chaos.
11. Stop worrying about who is to blame and seek understanding.
12. Learn that being alone is better than a bad relationship.
13. Find a way to avoid avoidable suffering.

14. Be resilient; if something doesn't work, find a new way of doing it.

15. Keep yourself safe.

16. If there is a high road, be on it.

17. Remind yourself constantly of why you are doing this.

18. Learn to say no.

19. As Winston Churchill once said, "Never, never, never, never, never, never, never, never, give up!"

20. Walk away from trouble.

21. Keep the fires of inspiration burning.

22. Reach out to others.

Extend compassion to yourself and others

We can all use a little more compassion. Begin by extending compassion to yourself. Buddha said: *You yourself, as much as anybody in the entire universe, deserve your love and affection.*

We often fall into the trap of being too hard on ourselves. We use our self talk to try to "motivate" ourselves by being very self critical. We yell at ourselves in the hope that we can improve or change "bad" behavior. The reality is that, in the long term, punishment does not change behavior, praise and compassion do. When we lash out at ourselves and criticize and demean ourselves and speak with self-loathing, we inhibit change. Putting ourselves down destroys the connection with ourselves that allows growth; we cannot maintain the position of observer and we lose the ability to facilitate our own healing. Extend compassion to yourself!

It is always well to remember that in this human experience, we are all trying to do as well as we can. There are a few sociopaths that truly do not and cannot care, but, on the whole, we are all trying to put forth our best self. Sometimes we do not do very well. Sometimes we all need to be forgiven. One addict stated: *I am so often in need of forgiveness that I do not dare withhold it from others. I give it freely in hopes it will be there for me when I need it.* Extend compassion and forgiveness to others!

Advanced Recovery Benchmarks

If you have gotten this far, you have accomplished a great deal. Wanting to use advanced recovery benchmarks from which to measure progress means you are working in advanced recovery—no small accomplishment! Here are the benchmarks of advanced recovery:

Completing Recovery Phase

The Recovery Phase is about change making or the remaking of ourselves so that we can live without our drug of choice. We have extinguished the emotional bond between our feelings and acting out. We have learned new life skills and emotional management skills, which allow us to participate in life in healthy, happy ways. We have moved closer to the Savior and feel His influence in our lives.

Again it is the continual presence of serenity that tells us when we are ready to move from Recovery to Maintenance. If serenity is our constant companion, we have made the changes that Recovery requires; we are ready for Maintenance.

Therapeutic Resolution of Underlying Issues

Therapeutic resolution of underlying issues can have amazing results for the addict. Often, when resolution is found, myriad behaviors fall away.

Jeanie was recovering from an alcohol addiction. One of the underlying issues for her was the physical and emotional abuse she suffered at the hands of her alcoholic father. She was very codependent and made bad relationship choices. Her friend kept harping at her about needing to set better boundaries. Jeanie never really got what her friend was talking about. As Jeanie progressed through therapy, began healing from her abuse and gaining new self-esteem, she came to value herself. She also became less codependent and made much better relationship choices. She set much better boundaries without knowing that was what she was doing. It just felt natural to do with her new healing. Codependency, self-esteem and relationship choices were never the central focus of her therapy, but all improved or fell away when the underlying issues were resolved.

Unresolved issues will always pull us toward our addiction. We can go forward much more efficiently without them.

Accomplishing Twelve Step work and starting over

The Twelve Steps are a work that is never done. Accomplishing them to the point of enjoying the promised blessings is a benchmark of recovery. The Twelve Steps, even after we attain a benchmark, can continue to bring us healing.

> *When Albert Einstein was administering a test in one of his teaching assignments, his graduate assistant noticed that the test looked familiar.*
>
> *"Dr. Einstein, isn't this the same test you gave last term?"*
>
> *"Yes," replied Einstein, "it is."*
>
> *"But how can you do that, give the same test two terms in a row?"*
>
> *"Because, [if they are learning], the answers change."*

So it is with step work. As we grow and heal, as our insight and understanding increases, our answers change. That pattern of growth can continue throughout our life. We need to revisit the steps often; we harvest healing each time we do.

Continued Serenity and Sobriety

When we started this journey, we learned that without sobriety there is no recovery. That truth never changes, and one of the benchmarks we look for in advanced recovery is the attaining of substantial time in sobriety. There is not a fixed date or amount of time, just a continued, one-day-at-a-time accumulation of sobriety without our drug of choice.

Perhaps the continued presence of serenity is an even more meaningful benchmark than sobriety. We achieve sobriety by not using and we achieve serenity by doing all the things that lead to the healing of recovery. If we have serenity, then we have moved away from our addictive thoughts and behaviors and are walking down a different street; truly living in the safe Waters of Recovery.

The Mighty Change of Heart

The capstone of recovery is the mighty change of heart. It is the culmination of our work. Moving away from the life of "I want what I want, when I want it," to a spiritually based life that seeks to keep the Savior's directive to *love the Lord thy God with all thy heart, with all thy soul, and with all thy mind.*

This is the first great commandment.

And the second is like unto it...love thy neighbor as thyself (Matthew 22:37-39).

When we move from the isolated, selfish life of addiction to the spiritual world of love and service to others, our heart undergoes a tremendous overhaul. Alma asks: *Have ye spiritually been born of God? Have ye received his image in your countenances? Have ye experienced the mighty change in your hearts?*

Then he asks the question about Maintenance: *If ye have experienced a change of heart, and if ye have felt to sing the song of redeeming love, I would ask, can ye feel so now?* (Alma 5:14, 26).

When we experience the mighty change, we are not translated directly into God's presence. Life and its challenges continue on. We remain human and susceptible to our humanness. (Hence Alma's question: *Can ye feel so now?*) Some are surprised that they are not perfected as part of the process. They are surprised that sometimes urges come back, or that from time to time, they feel tempted again. Those feelings do not indicate a failure in our recovery; such feelings do not mean our addiction is back. They come to remind us of where we have been and how far we have come. Turn those feelings over, say a prayer of gratitude and move on.

CHAPTER 4

The Waters of Recovery;
The Living Water

*W*e can only understand the joy of living in the Waters of Recovery by leaving our addiction and finding sanctuary in the
healing waters. We understand when we get there. It's the point where
we leave the chaos of our self-destruction and find the waters that surround Him. The 204 or so souls known as the people of Alma felt this
way about the area where they came to know the Savior. *The waters of
Mormon ... how beautiful are they to the eyes of them who there came to the
knowledge of their Redeemer; ...and how blessed are they, for they shall sing
to his praise forever* (Mosiah 18:30). When we read that scripture, some
2,100 years later, we just cannot comprehend, what the *how beautiful* of
this verse was like. We were not there, and we did not receive the ex-
quisite gift that they received there. Having that experience and gaining
that gift of knowing the Redeemer, changes you in a very profound way.
It opens a spiritual understanding and brings a gratitude and joy that
changes our heart. This perspective can be found in no other way.

Although we did not share the experience of Alma's people, we may
find a very similar transformation of our own in the Waters of Recovery. We can feel the same wonderful realization of coming to know our
Savior. When we fight and change and bring ourselves to Him, when we
can get close enough to Him to touch the hem of His garment, when

He can say *I see that your faith is sufficient that I should heal you* (3 Nephi 17:8), then we also will understand and know. We will say of the Waters of Recovery: *How beautiful are they ...to the eyes of them who there came to the knowledge of their Redeemer; ...and how blessed are they, for they shall sing to his praise forever.*

We are nearing the end of our task and nearing the end of the Recovery Highway yet, we still have a few things left undone, a few very important things to consider.

Cleaning Up the Mess: Making Amends

The wake of every addict is littered with lies, broken promises, veiled intentions, stealing and betraying love, and so on; it is an unending stream. Those choices have not been made without consequences in our lives. Elder Marvin J. Ashton said: *Our freedom to choose our course of conduct does not provide personal freedom from the consequences of our performances. God's love for us is constant and will not diminish, but he cannot rescue us from the painful results that are caused by wrong choices* (Ashton, 1990). Part of healing and reconciling the *painful results* is the process of making amends.

The alcoholic [addict] *is like a tornado roaring his way through the lives of others. Hearts are broken. Sweet relationships are dead. Affections have been uprooted. Selfish and inconsiderate habits have kept the home in turmoil* (Bill W. 2001).

When we *come to ourselves* and begin the healing process, we learn about amends; this means making reparations, restitution and reconciling with those we have harmed. By making things as right as possible, we free ourselves of the lingering consequences of our addiction. It is not an exact or complete science. Some things cannot be undone and things like virtue cannot be regained. In certain cases, more harm may be caused by our attempts at amends, but, to the extent possible, we must make efforts of reparation and restitution to those we have harmed. We must clean up our mess.

Some try to fudge and get by the efforts of making amends. They try to pass out adhesive bandages to people with serious wounds; they aren't interested in the work that healing serious wounds requires. They want it all to go away so they can get back to business as usual. That isn't going to be good enough. That isn't healing. This is where we need the broken heart and contrite spirit of godly sorrow that allows us to truly, honestly take responsibility for our actions and make amends.

The Old Testament has a law concerning repairing the damage we have caused: *If a soul sin, and commit a trespass against the LORD, and lie unto his neighbor ... or in a thing taken away by violence, or hath deceived his neighbour; Or have found that which was lost, and lieth concerning it, and sweareth falsely...*

Then it shall be...he shall even restore it in the principal, and shall add the fifth part more thereto, and give it unto him...

And he shall bring his trespass offering unto the LORD, a ram without blemish out of the flock, unto the priest...and...make an atonement for him before the LORD: and it shall be forgiven him...(Leviticus 6:1-7).

The law required not only that *he ... restore it in the principal,* but also that the offender *shall add the fifth part more thereto.* In addition, the sinner was required to *bring his trespass offering unto the LORD, a ram without blemish out of the flock.* The law required Israel to go beyond the original amount involved in the offense. We also should have the attitude of making things right by restoring more than we have harmed.

The results of our past shortcomings can become quite a burden for us. If we do not make amends and find reconciliation for them, they remain emotional markers that we owe. If our dark past is ignored and unattended to, those emotional debts impede our healing and recovery progress. They can slow or stop our growth.

As ships travel the seas, a curious saltwater shellfish called a barnacle fastens itself to the hull and stays there for the rest of its life, surrounding itself with a rocklike shell. As more and more barnacles attach themselves, they increase the ship's drag, slow its progress and decrease its efficiency.

Periodically, the ship must go into dry dock, where with great effort the barnacles are chiseled or scraped off. It's a difficult, expensive process that ties up the ship for days.

But not if the captain can get his ship to Portland (Oregon). Barnacles can't live in fresh water. There, in the sweet fresh waters of the Willamette or Columbia, the barnacles die and some fall away, while those that remain are easily removed. Thus, the ship returns to its task lightened and renewed.

Sins are like those barnacles. Hardly anyone goes through life without picking up some. They increase the drag, slow our progress and decrease our efficiency. Unrepented, sins build up one upon another; they can eventually sink us.

In His infinite love and mercy, our Lord has provided a harbor where, through repentance, our barnacles fall away and are forgotten. With our souls lightened and renewed, we can go efficiently about our work and His (Monson, 2000).

Repentance truly does *lighten and renew* our soul. The heavy burdens are stripped away and most importantly, forgotten. Part of the healing comes from our efforts at restitution, our amends. We need to make right our mistakes as best we can. Making amends helps clean off the barnacles of our past mistakes, which have built up and slow our progress. Making amends fits us for His service. It fits us for healing and recovery.

The sons of Mosiah *traveled throughout all the land of Zarahemla... zealously striving to repair all the injuries which they had done* (Mosiah 27:35).

We also must be zealous in striving to repair all the injuries that we have caused. The sons of Mosiah tried to find all those who they might have harmed. This process of making amends is not easy work. It is very humbling and can have a feeling of embarrassment that we must deal with. We must have Courage, Commitment and Accountability to honestly complete the task.

The Addiction Recovery Program Guide warns, however, that making direct restitution to all persons you have harmed is not a simple or easy job: *We needed courage, good judgment, sensitivity, prudence and appropriate timing. These were not qualities that most of us possessed at that time. We realized that step 9 would once more test our willingness to humble ourselves and seek the help and grace of the Lord* (LDS Family Services, 2005).

Sometimes, making amends seems beyond our ability, as it did for Ron:

Make amends? How do you make amends for infidelity, for betraying your promises? How do you fix it when you have nearly destroyed the one you love the most? How do you repair the shame created for your family? Children that you adore have lost their respect and like for you, because you have embarrassed them. They want nothing to do with you. How do you make amends for that? The financial ruin and loss of respect and friendships, how does all that get fixed? And then there is God, whom I turned away from and tried to ignore. All the sacred promises I made Him. How does all that go away?

Sounds like the poor fellow with the elephant on his plate that he is required to eat. *How do you do that? Where do you start? How do we do what is overwhelming, and apparently impossible?* The answer of wisdom is: *We do it a bite at a time.*

Time is a reoccurring requirement of recovery. Many of the steps we take, or the efforts we make, require time—often lots of it. This is not an easy requirement for someone who used to subscribe to the credo: *I want what I want, when I want it!* Patience and long suffering are not tools that an addict is familiar with. However, in recovery, they are essential. Patience and long suffering are learned skills grown in the garden of humility. Perhaps the gentle reminder that our family and the Lord have been patient and long suffering with us, while we were lost in our addiction, will strengthen our commitment and resolve.

Ron is well into his recovery now, but says:

It feels like I will be making my amends well into the next life. A lifetime doesn't feel like enough to repair some of the damage I have done, or some of the relationships I have destroyed.

But that is okay. I have started the process, and I try to work on it every day. I am amazed at what has been accomplished and I know I will get there when I get there. My job is to just keep working at it.

Remember Rule Number 1 from Early Recovery? *Shut up and do the work.* This rule carries the sense of being in the trenches and just doing our job. Just keep pluggin'. Plodding on. Moving forward. Day after day, hour after hour, doing the work of recovery, using the tools of recovery, observing the rules of recovery, healing the old wounds and repairing damage to others, will put you in good stead and in the position that all *shall be well with you.*

The Savior asks that if *ye shall come unto me, or shall desire to come unto me, and rememberest that thy brother has aught against thee—*

Go thy way unto thy brother, and first be reconciled to thy brother, and then come unto me with full purpose of heart, and I will receive you (3 Nephi 12:23-24).

The Lord wants us to make amends. He wants our slate clean when we come unto Him. He does not distinguish between a large offense and a small one. He only gives the direction that He will receive us after we make our amends with our brothers and are free of our burdens that impede our *full purpose of heart.*

Relationships: Rebuilding Trust

It does not even need to be said that if there has been an addict in the marriage, there have been relationship problems. Every relationship, not just the marriage relationship, has been damaged and affected. It is a given. Repairing the damage in all of our relationships is a mandatory amends for healing.

Respect is something that you feel for a person, because that person displays evidence that they are respectable—they behave in a manner that you can admire, honor or esteem. When you are in addict mode, you don't qualify.

Our ideal marriage involves things like trust, loyalty, fidelity and mutual respect; we treat each other with kindness and love and give support in the difficult times. The problem is that addicts are incapable of those behaviors, because they are much too busy being addicts. The spouse is often embarrassed by the addict's behavior, and the spouse comes to question the addict's ability to make decisions. Rather than feeling love and support, the spouse feels betrayal. So much for any chance of an ideal marriage.

The spouse they believed [in] *no longer exists to them. Spouses grieve that loss. They will experience shock, denial, pain, anger, and depression at different stages, sometimes all at once—this is a powerful and often overwhelming emotional state* (Coston, 2002).

My world has turned upside down. I can't even remember the ride home after our "disclosure session." I felt like I was in a haze for a week, just going through the motions. All of the information is just starting to come together for me. I fluctuate between wanting to forgive him and filing divorce papers. I have always been the "stable" one in our relationship, and recently that isn't the case (Carnes, 2008).

These quotes help illustrate the plight of spouses; they are in a very, very difficult place. We should respect that, take responsibility for ourselves and become the marriage partner they always thought we would be.

Some addicts in the Discovery Phase will vehemently deny that they are not holding up their end of the marriage.

I am always there for my wife and kids. Nothing gets in the way of that!

That is the addict's voice. It is the voice of denial. They often compound their sins by blaming the spouse for all problems. The reality is that someone active in their addiction is emotionally unavailable to participate in a relationship. If addiction is present, relationship damage will occur. It is inevitable. If blame must be handed out, it should go to the addict.

All of our interpersonal relationships should be built on a foundation of mutual respect, trust, and appreciation ... built on true values, openness, respect, trust, and understanding. Especially understanding (Ballard, 1998).

Living in a world that relies on the reality-bending benefits of denial and thinking errors can eliminate any chance of *respect, trust, openness or understanding.* It really takes a toll on our ability to maintain relationships. We do some funky thinking about what relationships should be like. Addicts almost universally come to believe that the only thing that stands between them and a happy, healthy relationship is their spouse. If they would only change how they behave, things would be fine.

The reality of healthy relationships is that the best way to make things better is to improve or change our own behavior. When we want the other person to change, we have moved into the need to control. It may be the understatement of the year to say that controlling behavior is never very helpful in relationships.

Addicts forget what healthy relationships are supposed to look like. One characteristic is that most anything can be talked about. There is no need for secrecy or hiding what we have done, feel or think. We don't feel the need to always be right. Often addicts don't care about the issue or even their stand on an issue, they only feel the need that when the argument or discussion is over, they are deemed to be right. Healthy relationships seek to find understanding and solutions and are not concerned with right or wrong or blame. Another quality of a healthy relationship is that there is no shame generated by the relationship on either side. There should be ample amounts of respect on both sides to achieve the sought after healthy status.

Good relationships are created using skills. These skills we can learn with effort and practice. While they do require work, they also produce great emotional benefits. They can fulfill our instinctual need to love and be loved and promote our sense of well-being while providing us with a secure, safe place in the world.

We should have a good enough relationship with ourselves that we can say; *It would be better to be alone than to be in a bad relationship.* We should have the confidence that even though it is painful to lose a relationship, we can survive and move on (Najavits, 2002).

Adding to the weight of the spouses' struggles is the sense of loss. Consider the dilemma of LDS individuals who have been married in the temple. They have expectations that involve the eternities. Their emotional safety involves covenants and promises they assume their partner has been keeping. There is tremendous shock and trauma in learning differently, in realizing our partner is not whom we thought they were. We realize we may be losing something very sacred to us. Our world comes crashing down. Often there is a grieving work to be done over that loss.

These profound challenges for the spouse may not leave much emotional capitol for love and support of the addict. The innocent spouse has every right and need to tend to themselves. The addict frequently cannot understand and is often resentful of the spouses' needs (that were induced by the addict's behavior), for time to heal. That is the addict still in addict thinking mode. Part of making our amends is doing what we can to facilitate the healing of those wounds for our partner. Allowing whatever that requires, whatever amount of time, space or effort, our responsibility is to supply it.

Given the burden our spouse must carry, we have no right to demand that our spouse be there for us in our recovery. Often the sequence goes like this for a porn addiction: addict gets caught, addict confesses (sometimes with reluctance) and goes to the Bishop. The addict feels euphoric and thinks the problem is solved. The addict gets way ahead of family members and friends who are still reeling from the revelation of addiction.

The addict is excited to be a new man (or woman) and is ready for, or expects (sometimes demands), forgiveness and support. The family members, however, may not be in a place where they are able to provide that. They are still trying to climb out of the crater of the bombshell that was dropped by the revelation of the addiction. They may still be in shock, and often they may feel that they have been living a lie.

When the addict says, "There isn't a problem any more," family members don't know what to believe. They believed and trusted, even placed their emotional and spiritual security with the addict while he pretended there was no problem. Does the addict really expect them to believe him now? Really?

President Hinckley presented a letter in General Conference Priesthood Meeting he had received from the troubled spouse of a long time porn addict:

Dear President Hinckley,

My husband of 35 years died recently. He had visited with our good bishop as quickly as he could after his most recent surgery. Then he came to me on that same evening to tell me he had been addicted to pornography. He needed me to forgive him [before he died]. He further said that he had grown tired of living a double life. [He had served in many important] Church callings while knowing [at the same time] that he was in the grips of this 'other master.'

I was stunned, hurt, felt betrayed and violated. I could not promise him forgiveness at that moment but pleaded for time.... I was able to review my married life [and how] pornography had...put a stranglehold on our marriage from early on. We had only been married a couple of months when he brought home a [pornographic] magazine. I locked him out of the car because I was so hurt and angry.

For many years in our marriage... he was most cruel in many of his demands. I was never good enough for him...I felt incredibly beaten down at that time to a point of deep depression.... I know now that I was being compared to the latest 'porn queen.'

We went to counseling one time and...my husband proceeded to rip me apart with his criticism and disdain of me...

I could not even get into the car with him after that but walked around the town...for hours, contemplating suicide. [I thought,] 'Why go on if this is all that my 'eternal companion' feels for me?'

I did go on, but zipped a protective shield around myself. I existed for other reasons than my husband and found joy in my children, in projects and accomplishments that I could do totally on my own ...

After his 'deathbed confession' and [after taking time] to search through my life, I [said] to him, 'Don't you know what you have done?'...I told him I had brought a pure heart into our marriage, kept it pure during that marriage, and intended to keep it pure ever after. Why could he not do the same for me? All I ever wanted was to feel cherished and treated with the smallest of pleasantries ... instead of being treated like some kind of chattel.

I am now left to grieve, not only for his being gone but also for a relationship that could have been [beautiful, but was not].

Please warn the brethren (and sisters). Pornography is not some titillating feast for the eyes that gives a momentary rush of excitement. [Rather] it has the effect of damaging hearts and souls to their very depths, strangling the life out of relationships that should be sacred, hurting to the very core those you should love the most.

President Hinckley continued with his own comments:

What a pathetic and tragic story. I have omitted some of the detail but have read enough that you can sense her depth of feeling. And what of her husband? He has died a painful death from cancer, his final words a confession of a life laced with sin (Hinckley, 2004).

There are no winners in stories such as these. The end results vary little from addiction to addiction. Unlike sexual addictions, some addictions lack the secrecy element, therefore, don't elicit the same shock that comes with revealing the addiction's presence. Still, all addictions create the same kind of relationship devastation. Spouses of alcoholics and drug addicts have their own special misery, aware that their lives are being slowly destroyed but feeling helpless to stop it. This story does give the addict a chance to glimpse the pain and suffering experienced by the spouse.

This kind of betrayal in the LDS world of eternal marriage commitment—where we strive to work together to build lives and families worthy of the Celestial Kingdom—is especially devastating. It attacks the sense of security and safety that our faith and covenants are supposed to build. Our defense in this wicked world is the idea that, together, we are safe, because we are righteous and working side by side. Then, for spouses of addicts, it is learned, often after many years, that they are not safe at all. This kind of traumatic revelation, challenging safety and security—which are among our most basic needs—can create devastating emotional struggles for the spouse. In the example above, the spouse mentions *stunned, hurt, felt betrayed and violated.* Add to that fear, anxiety, doubt, anger, frustration, embarrassment, loss, feeling used, belittled, depression, discouragement and the list goes on. The addict's behaviors can create emotional storms that are very, very difficult to weather.

Make the commitment to rebuild relationships. Don't base that commitment on anyone else's behavior. *Well if my wife doesn't forgive me, there is nothing I can do* is not a valid statement—that is more addict talk. Your job is to do everything in your power, regardless of how others respond at first. This is the place where patience and long-suffering can be very helpful. By consistent recovery effort, changes will come.

Katie Coston directs this advice to spouses who have had affairs, but it applies to all addicts:

Let me also warn you—your spouse may not jump for joy to hear that you've recommitted yourself to your marriage. If this is the case, realize that I may not mean that they don't want your marriage to be healed—it may mean that they just plain don't trust your behavior. You can make promises to anyone in the world about anything in the world—but your promises are meaningless unless you keep them—and you've already broken one signifi-cant promise that you made to them. Understand that it is natural for your spouse to feel distrust towards you, but their distrust for you is based on your past behavior, not your future behavior—it's going to take a little time for them to believe in your promises again (Coston, 2002).

Rebuilding trust starts with sobriety, the stopping of the addictive behavior. Stopping alone does not mean that everything is okay, and it does not mean that we can and should be trusted again. Rebuilding trust takes much more. Rebuilding trust requires more than the origi-nal gaining of trust. After all, we were found to be untrustworthy; why should trust again be extended to us? Rebuilding trust requires the evi-dence of change. It comes as we demonstrate the benchmarks of recov-ery. These announce that our lives are changing, that we former addicts have fundamentally and profoundly changed.

It is most likely that your spouse will not respond in a positive manner to your new behaviors at first, so expect your spouse's rejection. Your spouse is probably experiencing grief and grief is often an overwhelming emotional state. Because your spouse is overwhelmed with emotion—expect most of their choices to simply reflect their current emotion. Have patience and use repetition to further your example until your spouse trusts your new behavior and follows your lead.

- *Your spouse will learn to trust you, based on the consistency of your behavior.*

- *Your fortitude* [courage and commitment] *will determine your consistency.*

- *Your consistency will determine your spouse's level of distrust.*

- *If you want to heal your marriage, your spouse needs to feel respect for you.*

- *If your spouse is to feel respect for you, they must esteem your behavior.*

- *If you want your spouse to esteem your behavior, your behavior must be honorable* (Coston, 2002).

We should not be afraid to apologize, often. In our apologies we should acknowledge the pain we have brought to them and take responsibility for it. We should include assurances that this will not happen in the future. Our apologies should not be attached to any expectations on our part that they will be accepted and all will be forgiven. Forgiveness comes on our spouse's time table, not ours. Our language should sound like:

I know I have made bad choices that have hurt you I am not going to do that anymore. I am working very hard to change. I am sorry for the pain I have caused.

I was wrong to make the choices I did. I know they impacted you and have hurt you. I am not going to do that anymore. I am sorry that I hurt you.

I know you are angry with me and I deserve that. I am going to make up for all of this; I am sorry for my behavior.

This must be very hard for you and I am sorry I put you in this position. I should not have done that. I will not do that in the future.

DO NOT ASK FOR FORGIVENESS! In President Hinckley's story, the wife of the porn addicted husband said *He needed me to forgive him* this is the voice of an addict. When we say, Please forgive me and ask forgiveness, we are putting a burden on our spouse to forgive. This can force them into a position of guilt if they are unable to forgive at that moment. When we immediately ask for forgiveness, hoping to get off the hook, the spouse becomes the bad guy if they don't forgive. That is unfair. Forgiveness will come when we have proven through our life changes that we are worthy of that loving gift. It should not be requested until we have earned it.

The Mighty Change of Heart

The goal of recovery is the mighty change of heart. It is the healing of the soul. The people of King Benjamin described how the Spirit of the Lord *has wrought a mighty change in us, or in our hearts, that we have no more disposition to do evil, but to do good continually* (Mosiah 5:2), Alma asked this question: *Have ye spiritually been born of God? Have ye received his image in your countenances? Have ye experienced this mighty change in your hearts?* (Alma 5:14) This is the capstone of recovery.

When we have undergone this mighty change, which is brought about only through faith in Jesus Christ and through the operation of the Spirit upon us, it is as though we have become a new person. Thus, the change is likened to a new birth. Thousands of you have experienced this change. You have forsaken lives of sin, sometimes deep and offensive sin, and through applying the blood of Christ in your lives, have become clean. You have no more disposition to return to your old ways. You are in reality a new person. This is what is meant by a change of heart (Benson, 1989).

For the addict, a change of heart manifests as a loss of desire around the addiction. The urges and compulsions stop coming. Clinically, we would say the emotional bond between our emotions and our drug of choice has been extinguished. This freedom is found upstream of the waterfalls in the quiet Waters of Recovery. What is the *doing* of it? How is it accomplished? How does this mighty change come?

The scriptures are replete with passages that promise His help in healing us. He asks us to *purge ye out the iniquity which is among you;* [find and maintain sobriety] *sanctify yourselves before me* [do the work of recovery] (D&C 43:11). Sobriety alone is not enough. We must repent, make amends and find ways of living life in righteousness ways of living that invite His sanctification of us.

Lehi's words to his sons apply to the addict: *Awake my sons; put on the armor of righteousness. Shake off the chains with which ye are bound, and come forth out of obscurity, and arise from the dust* (2 Nephi 1:23). Again, by finding and maintaining sobriety, we can *shake off the chains* which bind us. Coming out of obscurity directs us to come to Him and to establish conscious contact with Him.

The gateway to Him is humility. *Be thou humble; and the Lord thy God shall lead thee by the hand and give thee answer to thy prayers* (D&C 121:10). And He promises to give us *knowledge by His Holy Spirit, yea, by the unspeakable gift of the Holy Ghost,* (D&C 121:26). Our part is to live in a way that is worthy of the Holy Ghost's presence and inspiration. We must search for His voice in our lives and seek His guidance. The Rules of Recovery outline the kind of behaviors that lead us to where we may hear the Holy Ghost.

He has said it plainly: *Fear not; for I am with thee: be not dismayed; for I am thy God: I will strengthen thee; yea I will help thee; I will uphold thee with the right hand of my righteousness* (Isaiah 41:10). He will *help* us and even *strengthen* us; we need only not fear or get lost in our frustrations and misguided expectations (*dismayed*).

We often want to define how He should heal us; and when things don't happen as we expect, we lose our faith. Over our own foolish expectations, we turn away from Him because we did not understand His ways. We lack His eternal perspective. We fail to use our *eye of faith* (Ether 12:19, Alma 5:15). And it is faith we must rely upon to achieve the healing we seek. Remember, faith and humility combine to produce sufficient Willingness for healing.

The mighty change of heart is simple we only need turn to Him, put our complete trust and faith in Him, and obey His will for us. It is by spiritually coming to God that we are healed, and this means coming with all of our *might, mind, and strength*. It is a fairly simple thing to explain, really, but the doing of this simple thing escapes many. That is because, besides the spiritual things we must do, we must also make some emotional, physical, behavioral and mental changes in how we manage our lives. It is our humanness that so often interferes with our spiritual efforts.

If we are suffering from emotional storms of anxiety, depression, fear, anger, resentment or jealousy, we struggle to find the Lord when we reach out to Him. Learning better ways to manage our emotions allows us to approach Him with all of our *might, mind, and strength*. When He tells us: *Be thou humble,* He is asking us to quiet the emotional storms and allow His spirit to direct us. Quieting the emotional storms takes faith and trust in Him. It also takes emotional management skills that help us not overreact to the emotional ups and downs of life.

Physically, we must take care of ourselves. He has said: *The elements are the tabernacle of God; yea, man is the tabernacle of God, even temples; and whatsoever temple is defiled, God shall destroy that temple* (D&C 93:35). Physically caring for our *tabernacle* prepares it for use as a temple. Obviously using drugs and alcohol defile the tabernacle. But we must do more than just not use; we must also be proactive in caring for and maintaining this facility we live in. Diet, exercise, healthy lifestyle, getting enough rest and medical visits are all efforts that help us make ready our tabernacle to become a temple.

We must move away from our addictive behaviors and into behaviors that take us to Christ. The keeping of the commandments, service and the living of the gospel of the Savior guide us to the changes we need to make behaviorally. In explaining how to use priesthood powers, the Savior taught us all how to live: *by long-suffering, by gentleness and meekness, and by love unfeigned; By kindness, and pure knowledge, which shall greatly enlarge the soul without hypocrisy, and without guile—Let thy bowels also be full of charity towards all men ... let virtue garnish thy thoughts unceasingly; then shall thy confidence wax strong in the presence of God...The Holy Ghost shall be thy constant companion ...* (D&C 121:41-46). So many of our human behaviors repel the Spirit and do not allow it to visit us. The qualities found in these verses invite it. When we display them, we are telling Him we are ready and worthy.

Mentally, we should manage our lives according to the instruction to *let virtue garnish thy thoughts unceasingly.* Anything that is not virtuous detracts from our goal. As we learn to become the observer, live in the moment and manage our self-talk we are preparing ourselves mentally for the mighty change. It has as much to do with getting rid of the mental activities that inhibit the Spirit as it does with replacing them with Spirit-inviting mental management.

When we make the appropriate changes emotionally, physically, behaviorally, and mentally, we are prepared to accomplish our spiritual goal of coming to Christ and experiencing the mighty change of heart.

President Eyring has taught: *That mighty change is reported time after time in the Book of Mormon. The way it is wrought and what the person becomes are always the same. The words of God in pure doctrine go down deep into the heart by the power of the Holy Ghost. The person pleads with God in faith. The repentant heart is broken and the spirit contrite. Sacred covenants have been made. Then God keeps His covenant to grant a new heart and a new life, in His time* (Eyring, 2004).

President Eyring taught us the five elements or stages of this process:

1. *God's words are carried deep into the heart by the Holy Ghost.*

2. *The person pleads with God in faith, exhibiting desire and faith.*

3. *There is a broken heart and contrite spirit (the presence of godly sorrow).*

4. *Sacred covenants and promises are made.*

5. *A new heart and life are given (with the understanding that it comes on His timetable).*

Our contribution to this process then becomes our ability to access the Holy Ghost and welcome it deeply into our heart. We need faith in Him and the desire to plead for this gift; we need the humility that creates the broken heart and contrite spirit. The efforts we make in recovery should all be preparing us to participate in this process. Whether it is gaining sobriety, living in the moment or establishing conscious contact with our emotions and our God, these are all steps designed to prepare us and to develop the abilities that bring this gift into our lives.

Finding the Gift in It

Ron related:

> My grandmother used to take me on her lap and share, "There is a gift in everything. Even your failures and disappointments, God sends you a gift, so that it is not in vain. Always look for the gift He has left you. It is up to you to

find it. It may feel hidden, but it will always be there." Over the course of life, I have found grandmother's wisdom to be true. There is blessing that can be born out of every suffering.

The sons of Mosiah *zealously went about* preaching the word and righting their wrongs after being visited by the angel. They had been *a great hinderment to the prosperity of the church of God: stealing away the hearts of the people; causing much dissension among the people; giving chance for the enemy of God to exercise his power over them* (Mosiah 27:9). They had sought to secretly work to destroy the church of God before the angel came.

His message was very direct. *Alma arise and stand forth, for why persecutest thou the church of God?* (Mosiah 27:13). The angel indicated that he came because of the faith and prayers of the people and his father, he declared his power and ended by saying to the young Alma, ... *Go thy way and seek to destroy the church no more, that their prayers may be answered, and this even if thou wilt be thyself be cast off* (Mosiah 27:16).

Alma and the sons of Mosiah chose to not be cast off. Their realization of what they had done drove them to be *zealously striving to repair all the injuries which they had done to the church. And thus they were instruments in the hands of God in bringing many to the knowledge of the truth, yea, to the knowledge of their Redeemer. And how blessed are they! for they did publish peace; they did publish good tidings of good; and they did declare unto the people that the Lord reigneth* (Alma 27:35-37).

In the end, the sons of Mosiah and Alma are not remembered for those misguided days of seeking to destroy the church, but they are remembered for their amazing missionary work and church leadership. They were driven by a regret of what they had done and those they had harmed. They felt a godly sorrow; it was the gift for them. Their weakness turned into a gift of great strength. They developed amazing testimonies from the wreckage of the unbelief of their youth, and those testimonies—their gift—led to the salvation of many. Our own suffering and failings can reap strengths for us and blessings for others.

We must constantly strive to do our best in emulating the Savior in every aspect of our lives. At the same time, however, let us remember that spiritual growth comes "line upon line," that the key—in the spirit world, as well as in mortality—is to keep progressing along the right path (Ballard 1987). Spiritual growth comes line upon line. Ponder what that infers. If all the line upon lines were stacked upon one another, at the top of the stack we would have true and complete spiritual understanding and we would know God. Most of us are not there spiritually. We are somewhere lower, buried in that stack, but trying to move up—that movement coming line upon line, of course.

In our addiction, we might find ourselves very low in the stack, perhaps very near the bottom. The same rules apply while we struggle in addiction; we must move up, line upon line, no matter how low our starting point is. Our goal is always the next line, to *keep progressing along the right path.* Don't worry about time or history; they don't matter. All that really matters—all that He really wants—is for us to move towards Him on this *right path.*

We are not told that we only progress line upon line if we are above a certain point in the stack or have reached a certain level of righteousness. There are no qualifiers. Wherever you are, simply find the next line and then the next, so that you also can build line upon line.

Some excuse themselves by saying they have done too much, or they think they are unworthy. If we do so, we deny ourselves His healing process. Or, perhaps, we withhold our help from others because we deem them too far gone. (They aren't high enough in the stack for us.) Or we pull away saying, *They have to hit bottom first.* These are all convenient excuses, but they are just excuses.

Father doesn't see it that way. He wants all to come, whatever their position, no matter if they lie near the bottom of the stack. He wants all to move towards Him. He wants them to come in this line upon line fashion. Each of us, no matter our history or situation, should take the next step before us. It is really the only one available to us. There is no line skipping. No free passes to the top of the stack, just the next line upon line.

We needn't be frustrated or dismayed by our lot or our place in the stack. If we get lost in the fear and anxiety of that, we miss the point. We miss what He wants for us. We miss what he desperately wants for us— which is to find the right path and then find the next line and the next and the next, all the way to Him.

There is only humble, step by step, line upon line healing and recovery. In the end, we will realize that it did not matter where we started; the important thing is that we made the journey, that we arrived where we needed to arrive.

We will not regret the past nor wish to shut the door on it. We will comprehend the word serenity and we will know peace. No matter how far down the scale we have gone, we will see how our experience can benefit others (Bill W 2001).

No matter how far down the scale you may be, you can always turn to Him. Reach out to Him. Move towards Him. It is promised that He is there. Many have found Him. He is anxiously waiting to hear from you.

Bibliography

Marvin J. Ashton, "A Pattern in all Things," *Ensign,* Nov 1990, 20.

Marvin J. Ashton, "The Measure of Our Hearts," *Ensign,* Nov 1988, 15.

M. Russell Ballard, "Building Bridges of Understanding," *Ensign,* Jun 1998, 62.

M. Russell Ballard, "Suicide: Some Things We Know, and Some We Do Not," *Ensign,* Oct 1987, 6.

Ezra Taft Benson, "A Mighty Change of Heart," *Ensign,* Oct 1989, 2.

Michael Bloch, http://www.worldwideaddiction.com. Accessed 8/17/09, 8:19 a.m.

Monte J. Brough, "A Willing Heart," *Ensign,* Nov 1988, 40.

Stephanie Brown, PhD, "About Addiction," *Counselor Magazine,* June 2006.

Patrick Carnes, PhD, *Don't Call it Love,* Bantam Publishing, New York,1992.

Patrick Carnes, PhD, *A Gentle Path Through the Twelve Steps,* Hazelden, Center City Minnesota, 1994.

Stephnie Carnes, PhD, *Mending A Shattered Heart,* Gentle Path Press, Carefree, Arizona, 2008.

Church Education System, *Old Testament Study Guide,* The Church of Jesus Christ of Latter-day Saints, Salt Lake City, Utah, 2002.

Spencer J. Condie, "A Mighty Change of Heart," *Ensign,* Nov 1993, 15.

Katie Coston, *Infidelity Crisis,* www.aftertheaffair.net, 2002.

Elaine Cannon, "Agency and Accountability," *Ensign,* Nov 1983.

Larry E. Dahl, "The Higher Law," *Ensign,* Feb 1991, 7.

Laura Davis, *The Courage to Heal Workbook,* Harper Collins Publishing, New York, 1990.

Dr. Wayne Dyer, *Getting in the Gap: Making Conscious Contact,* www.Inlight-times.com/ archieves/2005/02/dyer.htm. Accessed at 8/18/09, 9:30 p.m.

Henry B. Eyring, "As a Child," *Ensign,* May 2006, 14–17.

Henry B. Eyring, "The Book of Mormon Will Change Your Life," *Ensign*, Feb 2004, 9.

Henry B. Eyring, "Walk in the Light," *Ensign*, May 2008, 123–25.

Henry B. Eyring, "We Must Raise Our Sights," *Ensign*, Sep 2004, 14–19.

James E. Faust, "Choices," *Ensign*, May 2004, 51.

Terence Gorski, MA, *Denial Management Counseling*, Herald Publishing, New York, 2000.

Bruce C. Hafen, "The Atonement: All for All," *Liahona*, May 2004, 97–99.

Robert D. Hales. "We Can't Do It Alone," *New Era*, Jan 1977, 35-36.

Gordon B. Hinckley, "A Tragic Evil Among Us," *Ensign*, Nov 2004, 59-62.

Gordon B. Hinckley, "Living with Our Convictions," *Liahona*, Sep 2001.

Gordon B. Hinckley, *Teachings of Gordon B. Hinckley*, Deseret Book, Salt Lake City, 1997, 468.

Jeffrey R. Holland, "Broken Things to Mend," Ensign, May 2006, 69–71.

William Howatt, *The Human Services Counseling Toolbox*, Wadsworth Publishing, Belmont, CA, 1999.

Spencer W. Kimball, *Teachings of Presidents of the Church*: Church of Jesus Christ of Later-day Saints, Salt Lake City, 2006.

Spencer W. Kimball, *The Miracle of Forgiveness*, Bookcraft, Salt Lake City, 1969.

Dean L. Larsen, "Let Your Light So Shine," *Ensign*, Sep 1981.

Robert Larson MD, "Alcohol; The Substance, The Addiction, The Solution," Hazelden, Center City, MN,1998.

LDS Family Services, *Addiction Recovery Program*, The Church of Jesus Christ of Latter-day Saints, Salt Lake City, 2005.

LDS Bible Dictionary, The Church of Jesus Christ of Latter-day Saints, Salt Lake City, 1989.

The Latter-day Saint Woman: Basic Manual for Women, Part B, The Church of Jesus Christ of Latter-day Saints, Salt Lake City, 2000.

Abraham Maslow, *Toward a Psychology of Being*, John Wiley and Sons, New York, 1962.

Neal A. Maxwell, "How Choice a Seer!," *Ensign*, Nov 2003.

Neal A. Maxwell, "Why Not Now?" *Ensign*, Nov 1974, 12.

Neal A. Maxwell, "Meek and Lowly" *Ensign*, Oct 1987, 94.

John McCain, Mark Salter, *Why Courage Matters*, Random House, New York, 2004.

William Miller, Stephen Rollnick, *Motivational Interviewing*, The Guilford Press, New York, 2002.

Thomas S. Monson, "'Called to Serve'," *Ensign*, Nov 1991, 46.

Thomas S. Monson, "Great Expectations" (Church Educational System fireside for young adults, Jan. 11, 2009), www.ldsces.org)

Thomas S. Monson, "Your Eternal Voyage," *Ensign*, May 2000, 46.

Lisa M. Najavits, *Seeking Safety*, The Guilford Press, New York, 2002.

Portia Nelson, *There's a Hole in my Sidewalk; The Romance of Self-discovery*, Beyond Words Publishing Company, Hillsboro, OR, 1994.

Dennis B. Neuenschwander, "The Path of Growth," *Ensign*, Dec 1999, 13.

Dallin H. Oaks, "Our Strengths Can Be Our Downfall, *Ensign*, Oct 1994, 11.

Mary O'Malley, *The Gift of Our Compulsions*, The New World Library, Novato, CA, 2004.

Belleruth Napasstek, *Invisible Heroes*. Bantam Dell, New York, 2004.

Boyd K. Packer, "Self Reliance," *Ensign*, Aug 1975, 88,89.

Scott Peck, MD, *Further along the RoadLess Traveled*, Simon and Schuster, New York, 1993.

Ronald Potter-Efron. Patricia Potter-Efron, *Letting Go of Shame*, Hazelden, Center City, MN, 1989.

Stephan L. Richards, *Conference Report* 1954, 12.

Don Miguel Ruiz, *The Four Agreements*, Amber-Allen Publishing, San Rafael, CA, 1997.

Richard G. Scott, "Do What is Right" *Liahona*, March 2201.

Sexaholics Anonymous, *The White Book*, SA Literature, Brentwood, TN, 2002.

Marilyn J. Sorensen, PhD, *Breaking the Chain of Low Self-Esteem*, Wolf Publishing Co, Sherwood, OR, 1998.

Eckhart Tolle, *Practicing the Power of NOW*, New World Library, Navato, CA, 1999.

Kathleen Tomlin, Helen Richardson, *Motivational Interviewing and Stages of Change*, Hazeldon, Center City, MN, 2004.

Dieter F. Uchtdorf, "A Matter of a Few Degrees," *Ensign*, May 2008, 57-60.

Dieter F. Uchtdorf, "The Way of the Disciple," *Ensign*, May 2009, 75–78.

Dieter F. Uchtdorf, "The Infinite Power of Hope," *Ensign*, Nov 2008, 22.

Bill W., *Big Book*, AA World Services, New York, 2001.

Joseph B. Wirthlin, "Press On," *Liahona*, Nov 2004.

World Health Organization, *Health Education in Self-care: Possibilities and Limitations*. WHO, Geneva, 1983.

About the Author

Roger Stark is a person of recovery. He has walked the road of recovery. He has seen addiction from the inside. He has experienced the devastation to every facet of life that comes with the "disease". He also knows the healing that comes from leaving addictive behaviors behind and finding again the Savior.

Roger is also a trained and licensed addition counselor in the State of Washington. He is a clinician devoted to addiction recovery. He has worked and had private practice in a variety of settings with a wide range of clients.

When I was lost in my addiction, I uttered a simple prayer of pleading for help. I promised that if healing came to me, If I could find the way, I would help others find it also. He did not forget my promise, nor have I. This book and my practice are the result.

You may contact Roger, and order copies of this book, through his website: www.waterfallconcept.org